Sick and Tired

of

Being Broke

The First Steps on the Road to Financial Independence
for
"Everyday People"

By Lucille Tyler-Baldwin

Copyright © 2010 by Lucille Tyler-Baldwin

ISBN 0-7414-5821-7

Printed in the United States of America

Published February 2010

INFINITY PUBLISHING
1094 New DeHaven Street, Suite 100
West Conshohocken, PA 19428-2713
Toll-free (877) BUY BOOK
Local Phone (610) 941-9999
Fax (610) 941-9959
Info@buybooksontheweb.com
www.buybooksontheweb.com

Dedication

In honor of my grandparents:

Nellie and Walter Tyler

*

**This Book
is Dedicated
to**

The Tyler Family

*Through life's journeys our names may change,
but our souls will remain forever*
entwined.

*

The Use of Knowledge Is Powerful.

**To Seek It
Will Be Our Strength.**

Acknowledgments

Writing this book has been a dream of mine for many years. I spent most of those years procrastinating, instead of putting my dream on paper. My family, coworkers, and friends listened to me talk about my dream for years; someday, one day, I would say. I would talk to anyone that would listen about the importance of saving money and getting out of debt.

The greatest thing about family and true friends is that they give unconditional love and support, and for that I am eternally grateful. During my years of dreaming, they never seemed to tire of my constant talk about financial freedom or about a book that I never started. They always allowed me to go on and on and listened with a smile and an encouraging word.

To all my family, friends, and coworkers, I thank you sincerely. Your support and encouragement have meant more to me than you will ever know, and I love you all...

With special thanks to:

Pauline Tyler
Monique and Christina Baldwin
Alia Manning
Samuel Williams
Walter and Sheldon Tyler
Nicholas Jordan Baldwin
and
Victoria Snowten-Baldwin

Disclaimer

I am not a financial advisor or hardly an expert when it comes to money. What I *am* is a divorced mother of two who was "Sick and Tired of Being Broke" and decided to take charge of my life and to seek financial independence. On my journey I realized that we *all* have the right and the power to become financially independent. It does not matter if you are a janitor, a server, a teacher, or the CEO of a corporation — the road to financial independence is in your path. I also realized that our choices, and not our income, are what determine our destiny.

The road to financial independence is paved with information. It is important to seek out that information in as many forms as possible and not depend on one person or source. I encourage you to seek out the help of professionals in the field such as financial advisors, accountants, or lawyers before you take the steps outlined in this book.

This book is a recounting of my financial journey. It is the information and experiences that crossed my path along the way and should not be considered professional advice. The purpose of this book is to share with you the first steps on my journey to becoming financially independent. My hope is that together, one book at a time, one bill at a time, and one dollar at a time, we will find the information that we need to become free from debt.

Table of Contents

Introduction   *Changing a Conditioned Mind*   *11*

Chapter 1   *Getting Started: Your Credit and You*   *17*

Chapter 2   *You Can Afford to Save! Finding Your Wasted Wealth*   *51*

Chapter 3   *A Loyal Employee: Putting Your Found Money to Work*   *83*

Chapter 4   *Taking Charge: Learning to Become the Boss of Your Money*   *113*

Chapter 5   *Running Your Household: What You Don't Know Can Cost You!*   *157*

Chapter 6   *Breaking the Cycle: Your Kids and Money*   *169*

Introduction

<u>Changing a Conditioned Mind</u>

Conditioning is to train to behave or to become accustomed to behaving in a certain manner.

- however -

"We cannot solve problems by using the same kind of thinking we used when we created them."

Albert Einstein

Taking the first step on the road to financial independence will be the most difficult step of the journey. Changing a conditioned mind is more than changing your way of thinking; it is also changing your behavior. It is easy to sit back, complain, and do nothing to improve your life. Change takes work, sacrifice, and rethinking old ways. Change means taking charge of your life and developing better habits. Changing your life is only possible if you want to change and are willing to do the work.

I have friends who have been struggling financially for years. They want their financial life to improve; unfortunately, they do not want it enough to do the work. I have always wanted a tight, flat stomach so that I could wear a belly ring and stroll on the beach. I have always wanted to speak Spanish fluently, but I have never wanted either one enough to do the work. If you really want something, you have to want it enough to do the work.

Before you can take that first step on the road to financial independence, taking a step back may be necessary. We are all products of our childhoods, so we drag around our experiences like an old blanket, clean or dirty, into the future. Our experiences and the information that we received, or did not receive, may hold the key to our financial habits and the way that we view money. The child in us will continue to make decisions for us, unless we let go of the past and allow the adult in us to take charge.

Unfortunately, for most Americans, basic financial information is not taught in schools. We live in a country that continues to pass out diplomas to people who lack healthy financial skills, creating a society not prepared to handle the financial ups and downs of everyday living.

With financial education missing from our schools, it has been left up to the parents to teach their children how to handle money. Our system leaves this important task to parents who have little savings and are overwhelmed with debt. How can we expect parents to pass down information that they did not receive? If the parents were not taught to succeed financially, the chances are great that the children will not be prepared. The cycle will continue, creating another generation of people lacking financial power.

Growing up, I was aware that the adults around me went to work every day, paid the bills, and took care of our needs. They treated finance as a private matter and did not discuss money around the house. So, as a child, I was left to start piecing together my own views about money.

I picked up my first piece of the puzzle when I went to church on Sundays. I taught myself that not having money was okay because the Lord loved the meek. Matthew 5:5 states, *"Blessed are the meek, for they shall inherit the earth."* I do not know why those ten words stuck in my head, but they helped to form my views about money and wealth. Listening to those words with a child's ear, I took them to mean that not having money and wealth was a good thing. I thought it meant that I would be one of the special people that would receive my riches when I walked through the Pearly Gates.

To reinforce my thinking that not having extra money was normal, through the magic of television Jimmie Walker entered my life (best known as J.J. Evans or "Kid Dy-no-mite," from the TV show *Good Times*). The Evans family was a poor but loving family that struggled to make it financially. As hard as they tried, they could never make ends meet or get ahead. Growing up with the influences of the Evans family and other shows like it taught me that to struggle with money was normal. Negative influences, combined with a lack of financial information, put me on the road to paycheck-to-paycheck living. Because of those negative influences I wrongly assumed it was my destiny.

The Death of Financial Freedom:
Hanging on to old excuses

The best way to continue living paycheck-to-paycheck and to struggle financially is to hang on to old excuses.

Average List of Excuses

"I cannot afford to save money. I have too many bills."

"I do not have any extra money."

"Everyone has debt."

"I only spend money on things that I need."

"When I get my next raise, I will start saving."

"I need to take out another payday loan."

"I need my credit cards for emergencies."

"Only rich people can afford to save money."

"Times are too hard to save right now..."

Excuses can be never-ending and last a lifetime. To make matters worse, we unknowingly pass down those excuses to our children, giving them ready-made reasons to struggle financially.

Albert Einstein said that the definition of insanity is "doing the same thing over and over and expecting different results." The only way to achieve different results is to rethink and change what we are doing that is not working. The average American is carrying five to ten credit cards and depending more on borrowed money. The insanity is that *not* saving money for a rainy day has become the standard rule instead of the exception; spending every dollar we earn, and more, is common. The savings rate for the average person in this country is less than 1% of their income.

This formula of spending more than we earn and not saving is insanity. Waiting for someone to come along and save us from financial chaos is insanity; that person is not coming. Our government is in debt; banks needed a bailout; the average American is in debt, and still our schools are not teaching financial education — that is insanity. Since we cannot depend on someone else to save us, our only option is to educate and save ourselves.

If you are sick and tired of working all week just to pay bills, then the time for change is now. If you are sick and tired of having no savings in your time of financial need, then the time for change is now. If you are tired of the early morning telephone calls and late notices, then the time for change is now. If you are sick and tired of being broke, then the time for change is now.

The good news is that we are surrounded by financial information. By using the power of the Internet we can search the world for information that will benefit us. There are book stores such as Barnes & Noble and Books-A-Million that make it enjoyable to seek out information. We have access to free public libraries full of financial information and staffed with friendly people eager to help. Ask yourself: Do you want your life to be better? Do you want the lives of your children and their children to be better? I do.

The only person that can stop you from improving your life is you. The time for change is now, but change is only possible if you are willing to do the work. If you believe your only option is to struggle financially, then you will continue to struggle. If you believe that living paycheck-to-paycheck is your destiny, then you will continue to depend on your next check. If you believe, however, that change is possible, then your life will change. Changing your life is only possible if you want to change and are willing to do the work. Your actions will follow what your mind believes.

Chapter One

Getting Started:

<u>Your Credit and You</u>

"When you know better, do better."

Maya Angelou

My Goal:
<u>Stopping the Bill Collectors</u>

When my journey began, my goal was not to become financially independent, but to stop the bill collectors from calling my home. I can remember waking up early one morning from the sound of the telephone ringing. It was as I feared: another bill collector calling, wanting to know when they could expect a payment. I dreaded hearing the sound of my telephone ringing for many years. It is amazing how something as simple as a phone ringing could have the power to cause so much stress. It was that particular call, however, that would change my life.

The stress of the telephone calls that started every morning, combined with the late notices, had begun to take its toll on my nerves. When I sat up in bed that day, something in my soul stirred and my eyes began to sting as they filled with tears. I could feel my neck and my throat tighten, as I fought to hold back those tears and the urge to cry. It was at that moment that I was sick and tired of being broke. I didn't know how, but I knew that things would change.

I was not only sick and tired of the late notices and the calls, but also somewhere deep in my soul I was tired of my lifestyle. I was sick and tired of taking it one day at a time. I was sick and tired of working every day just to pay bills. I was sick and tired of being afraid when I heard a strange sound coming from under the hood of my car because I knew that I did not have the extra money for car repairs.

I was sick and tired of the stress that living paycheck-to-paycheck can cause. I had to ask myself, "How do I get the bill collectors to stop calling me?" The answer was simple: *pay them*! The answer may have been simple, but it took work and time for me to get out of debt. The only good thing about having debt is that it makes you appreciate not having it.

"When You Know Better, Do Better"

On my journey, I came across several articles and surveys that stated that only a small percentage of Americans know their credit score, or the importance of their credit report. Until recently, I was clueless about my own credit information. I was making important financial decisions for my household, and I had never heard of a credit report or FICO score. The articles and surveys published each year prove that there is a need for money management training in this country.

When I was working to get out of debt, I often heard Oprah Winfrey quote Maya Angelou, saying, "When you know better, do better." During that phase of my journey, I would sometimes become angry with myself because of my poor financial choices. "When you know better, do better" has become one of my favorite inspirational quotations. It reminded me that I could not afford to waste time stressing over the mistakes I made in the past because of financial ignorance.

I would become angry with the creditors for increasing my already-high interest rates and fees, when I was working so hard to get out of debt. I had to remind myself that *I* gave them power over me because I owed them money. I gave them the power to charge me high interest rates and fees because *I* failed to handle my business. *I* failed to read the contracts that I signed. *I* failed to live within my means and prepare for the unexpected. I gave them power because I borrowed their money.

"When you know better, do better." I would replay those words in my head to help me reach my goal. Those words were the motivation that I needed to push me forward and to help me focus on my destination. Learning better eventually gave me the power to start doing better.

The Power of Your Credit:
<u>Getting to Know It</u>

When I learned to drive, my mother would always tell me that if I got lost I should stop driving. I should figure out where I was so that I could get back on the right road. She would often tell me that if I continued to drive, it would only take me farther from my destination.

On my journey to financial independence, I stopped driving; I finally realized that I was going in the wrong direction. I had to stop creating debt, regroup, and get back on the right road. Your credit information is like a financial map telling you where you are and where you have been. It is the starting point to help you get back on the right road to reach your goal.

Credit Score

What is a credit score?

A Credit Score, also known as a <u>FICO</u> (Fair Isaac Corporation) score, is a three-digit number that is calculated based on your credit/payment history. It ranges from 300 to 850.

(Note: There is also another score called a Vantage Score. A Vantage Score can range from 501 to 990 but may not reflect your true score.)

What is the purpose of a credit score?

The purpose of your Credit Score is to help lenders determine if they should extend credit or lend money to you. To put it simply, the lender wants to have an idea of just how likely you are to repay their money. Your score will also determine how much you pay for a loan (interest rate). A low score may mean that you are too much of a risk, and your loan request could be turned down.

What determines my credit score?

Five factors determine your Credit Score; the two most important factors are your payment/credit history and how much you currently owe.

1. <u>Thirty-five (35) percent</u> of your credit score is based on your <u>payment history</u>. Your payment history shows a creditor if you have a habit of paying your bills late or on time. It also tells a creditor if you have bills that have not been paid and have been sent to collection agencies. Repossessions (even if you return a car or another item, it is still considered a repossession) or bankruptcies in your credit history

will hurt your score. The more recent the negative information, the worse it is for your score.

2.   Thirty (30) percent of your credit score is based on your outstanding debt: how much credit you have available and how much of it you are using. Your debt includes how much you owe on your credit cards, an auto loan, or your home loan. Having too many credit cards at or near their limits will hurt your score. A balance of 25% or less of your cards' limits are recommended. Having learned the hard way, I recommend only charging what you can pay when the bill arrives.

Your debt-to-income ratio is very important; think of it as a scale. If you put your debt on one side of the scale and your income on the other side, which side would weigh more? To keep your head above water, you want to have more income than debt. Drowning in debt means you have more debt than income.

3.   Fifteen (15) percent of your credit score is based on how long you've had credit. The longer you've had good credit established, the better it is for your credit score. A long history of poor credit, however, will affect your credit score in a negative way. Don't worry; you can work at improving your credit score.

4.   Ten (10) percent of your credit score is based on the number of inquiries. Going loan shopping is not good for your credit score. Applying for too many credit cards or loans may tell a lender that you are in trouble financially or that you are about to take on a lot of debt. So, no more going from loan company to loan company, that negative activity will show up on your credit report!

The next time a company offers you a free t-shirt, a

cheap umbrella, or a two-liter bottle of soda to apply for a credit card, run, don't walk. That so-called free gift could cost you a lower credit score or additional debt. Value and protect your credit.

5.   <u>Ten (10) percent</u> of your credit score is based on the <u>types of credit that you have</u>, meaning the types of loans you have such as student loans, credit cards, auto or home loans, etc. You should think of your credit score as money, because it can save you or cost you a great deal of money. Your credit score can determine whether you can get a loan to buy furniture, a car for work, or financing to buy a home for your family. Your credit score also determines the interest rate that you will be charged to buy those items. Remember: A low credit score will cost you $$. A high credit score will save you $$.

What does not affect my credit score?

By U.S. law, certain things are prohibited from being used for credit scoring:

- Your race, color, religion, national origin, sex, or your marital status.

- If you receive public assistance, or if you are exercising your rights under the Consumer Credit Protection Act.

(The Consumer Credit Protection Act protects employees from being fired by their employers because their wages have been legally seized/garnished for any one debt. It also limits the amount of money that can be garnished in any one week. For additional information about your rights as an employee, go to the United States Department of Labor's website at http://www.dol.gov/.)

- Your age (Other types of scores may consider your age, but the FICO score does not.)

- Your income, occupation, job title, hire date, employment history, and your employer are not used in your credit scoring, although it may be necessary for lenders to use this information, as well as other types of scores.

What is considered a good credit score?

The Fair Isaac Corporation's (FICO) score is the most commonly used formula, ranging from 300 to 850.

Those that have scores over 760 will get the best interest rates.

The lowest score typically needed to qualify for a low-cost mortgage is around 700.

Scores below 600 are normally charged a higher interest ("sub-prime") rate because they may not qualify for a prime rate. You may want to consider working to improve your score if it is below 600. The goal is to eventually have excellent credit.

FICO SCORE TIER
```
-----------------------------------------------------------
     500  590  625  660  690  720

     589  624  659  689  719  850
-----------------------------------------------------------
```

If your score is below 600 or even 500, do not be discouraged. You can take steps to improve your score. You can, however, expect to pay outrageous interest rates and possible fees if you are approved for credit at all. Purchasing a home may have to be put on hold until you bring up your score.

Armed with, and understanding, your credit information may give you the power to negotiate the best interest rate or to walk away from a bad offer. Knowing your score and increasing it by a few points may push you into a higher scoring bracket, and that means you *may* qualify for a more favorable interest rate. For example, if your score is 688, you are just a few points away from saving a great deal of money.

The good news is that no matter how low your credit score, with work and time, you can one day be in a higher FICO/Credit Score bracket. It will not happen overnight, but it is possible. Your Credit Score is **POWER**: take charge of it!

Credit Report

What is a credit report?

A credit report is like a report card from the lenders that you borrowed money from or lenders who have extended you credit; this includes your past and current credit activities. Your report includes your account balances and shows if you make payments on time. Your credit report will also show if any action was taken against you for unpaid bills. For example, if lenders sent any accounts to collection agencies or if you have any repossessions for nonpayment.

What is in my credit report?

The format may be different, but credit reporting agencies basically supply the same categories of information:

- **Identifying Information**

    Your name and any aliases

    Your addresses (previous and current)

    Your Social Security number

    Your date of birth

    Your employment information

These items on your credit report are updated with information that you supply to lenders. This information does not affect your credit score.

- **Trade Lines/Credit Accounts**

Each time you open and establish an account with a lender, the lending institution reports a number of things to credit reporting agencies:

The type of account you opened: i.e., bank card, auto loan, student loan, mortgage, etc.;

The date you opened or closed the account;

Your credit limit or loan amount;

Your account balance and your payment history.

• **Credit Inquiries**

Each time you apply for a loan or credit card, you authorize a lender to ask for a copy of your credit report. The inquiries section contains a list of those lenders. Authorizing a lender access to your credit report should only be given when you are ready and able to do business with that institution. Your credit report contains important and valuable information and should not be given out lightly.

• **Public Record Information**

Public records are also shown in your credit report. State and county records, information on any tax liens, bankruptcies, or monetary judgments are included.

The Value of Your Signature:
"Should I Co-sign a Loan?"

To co-sign or not is a very important decision that can affect your credit report. The person asking you to co-sign is likely a family member, spouse, or friend. Someone that you are dating may also put pressure on you to co-sign a loan. Since co-signing can affect your credit in a positive or negative way, it is not something to do without careful consideration.

You should think of co-signing as *co-buying* because you will be responsible for repaying the loan if they cannot or do not repay it. Can you afford to pay for a car? Can you afford to pay for a flat screen television or washer and dryer? Can you afford to repay a $5,000 loan? Do you want to become *legally liable* even if you can afford to repay the loan?

Depending on the state you live in, the creditor may come after *you* first for repayment of the loan instead of the primary borrower. Not only could you be responsible for repaying the loan but also for any late fees, collection costs, and attorney's fees. You could lose your property if you used it as collateral to secure the loan. The creditors may also try to sue you or garnish your wages for repayment.

Co-signing may also tie up your available credit, because lenders consider these additional debt obligations, and *until the loan is paid, they are!*

"Why Do They Need a Co-signer?"

- Do they have bad credit because of nonpayment or slow payment?

- Do they have good credit but their credit experience is only with small dollar amount loans?

- Do they lack a credit history because this is their first loan?

- Do they have good credit, but their income is low?

- As an alternative can you afford to give money instead of co-signing?

If You Decide to Co-sign/Co-buy:

- Will they allow you to review their credit report?

- Will they allow you online access to the account?

- You should request to have duplicate statements mailed to your home.

Keep in mind that if they pay on time and pay the loan back in full, it is a plus for your credit. If they make late payments or do not repay the loan, it will have a negative effect on *your* credit. If they need a co-signer because they have bad repayment habits, you should ask yourself one final question: if they do not value and respect their credit, why would they respect your credit?

How do I get a copy of my credit report?

Once each year, by U.S. law, you are entitled to request a FREE copy of your credit report. Beware! Many companies charge a fee for this information when it is available to you for *free* every year.

There are three main credit reporting bureaus: TransUnion, Experian, and Equifax. To receive your free copies, contact each of the three main credit bureaus by phone, mail, or go to the official website at www.annualcreditreport.com.

To contact the three main credit bureaus by phone or mail:

Equifax
P.O. Box 105873
Atlanta, GA 30348
http://www.equifax.com
1 (800) 685-1111

TransUnion
Consumer Disclosure Center
P.O. Box 1000
Chester, PA 19022
www.transunion.com
1 (800) 916-8800 or 1 (800) 888-4213

Experian
P.O. Box 2104
Allen, TX 75013-2104
www.experian.com
1 (800) 682-7654

Your credit report does not include your credit score, but it is available for a reasonable fee when you get your credit report.

A Basic Summary of
Your Rights Under the
<u>Fair Credit Reporting Act (FCRA)</u>

Before you get started, you should know that as a consumer you do have rights under the Fair Credit Reporting Act. There are consumer groups and agencies that have your best interest in mind and are set up to help you *"help yourself."*

The following information is only a small sample of your basic rights. For more information and additional rights, go to www.ftc.gov/credit or you can write to:

Consumer Response Center, Room 130-A
Federal Trade Commission
600 Pennsylvania Avenue N.W.
Washington, D.C. 20580

- You have the right to be informed if information in your file has been used against you.

- You have the right to know what is in your file.

- You have the right (for a fee) to know your credit score.

- You have the right to dispute information that you feel is inaccurate or information that may be incomplete. You have the right to report the inaccurate information to the reporting agency. As long as your dispute is not frivolous, the agency must investigate (sample dispute letter available on page 43 and at www.ftc.gov/credit).

- You have the right to expect consumer reporting

agencies to correct or delete inaccurate information, normally within 30 days. This includes information that is incomplete or negative information about you.

- You have the right to expect that consumer reporting agencies will not report outdated, negative information about you (negative information that is more than seven years old and 10 years for bankruptcies).

- You have a right to expect that consumer reporting agencies will limit access to your file to people who have a valid need to see your personal information.

- You have a right to expect a reporting agency not to provide information to your employer or potential employer, unless you give your consent in writing.

Once again, for additional information about your rights under the Fair Credit Reporting Act, go to: www.ftc.gov/credit.

Poor Financial Choices or a Financial Crisis
Does Not = Disrespect

Poor financial choices or a financial crisis beyond your control does not give anyone the right to talk to you or treat you with disrespect. During the process of getting your financial situation under control, hold your head high and be proud that you are taking your first steps to becoming debt free.

Do not feel that you are going through this process alone. There are a lot of people and agencies on your side that are fighting for you and your rights. The Fair Debt Collection Practices Act (FDCPA) was passed in 1977 by Congress in response to abusive practices by some bill collectors. The purpose of the FDCPA is to set guidelines for agencies collecting legitimate debts and to provide protection for those of us who owe money.

The Fair Debt Collection Practices Act protects us against:

- Collectors using profane language or behavior;

- Collectors threatening us with harm, including our property and reputation;

- Collectors using derogatory terms when addressing us (they are not allowed to address a letter: "Non-paying Lucy);

- Collectors sending postcards (postcards are not private);

- Collectors not identifying themselves when they call;

- Collectors making false statements.

Debt collectors are restricted by the FDCPA from:

- Contacting a third party concerning your debt, unless they are a co-signer. They are allowed to contact your neighbor, employer, or family member; but only to find out where you live, where you work, or your telephone number.

- Making false threats to scare you into paying your debt. They cannot *pretend* they are going to garnish your wages or have you arrested.

- Calling you at unreasonable times, like 5:00 a.m. A reasonable time is normally defined as not before 8:00 a.m. and not after 9:00 p.m., unless you give them permission.

- Calling you at work, if they are informed that it is against policy. If a bill collector calls you at work, the FDCPA does not allow them to inform your employer of the reason for the call, unless your employer asks the reason for the call *first*.

This is just a very small sample of your rights. For complete and detailed information about your rights under the Fair Debt Collection Practices Act, go to: www.ftc.gov.

The FTC, established in 1914, stands for the Federal Trade Commission. The FTC's Bureau of Consumer Protection works for the consumer to prevent fraud, deception, and unfair business practices in the marketplace. To learn more about the FTC, go to: www.ftc.gov. There are many people and agencies working to protect and educate us. We owe it to them, ourselves, and our families to absorb as much information as we can to make our lives better. We sometimes complain about our government, but they provide a wealth of information to us for free. The information is out there, waiting for us to turn off our television sets and take an interest. The use of knowledge is powerful: seek it and then share it.

Credit Repair:
<u>There Is No Magic Wand!</u>

No matter how much we wish, when it comes to repairing your credit, you cannot wave a magic wand and expect bad credit to disappear. People will prey on your stress and fears, and make promises that they cannot legally keep. Some unethical credit repair clinics use illegal tactics like stealing the credit files or Social Security numbers of minors or people that have died.

Some clinics even promise to erase bad, but accurate, credit by challenging every negative item in your file. If negative but accurate information is removed, it will reappear when the credit bureau receives affirmation from your creditor, usually within 30 to 60 days. Depending on the type of debt, negative but correct information can legally remain on your report for seven to ten years.

There are also clinics that will try to get you to create a new credit identity by applying for an employer identification number (EIN). This number is similar to a Social Security number; creating a number to avoid credit problems is illegal.

We have become conditioned to expect instant gratification: whatever we want with the swipe of a credit card, lunch or dinner without leaving our vehicles, weight loss in a pill. As much as we would like to believe otherwise, no one can legally remove accurate information from our credit report. There is no easy fix. You did not create debt overnight, and no one can magically make it disappear.

Do not be fooled or tempted by advertisements promising instant credit repair. There is no credit repair in a bottle. You can save yourself wasted time and hundreds, or even thousands, of dollars. The best way to clean up your credit is to take charge and arrange to repay what you owe.

A Credit Repair Clinic

or

<u>Do It Yourself?</u>

According to FCRA, everything that a credit repair clinic can legally do to repair your credit, you can do yourself. The information that a credit repair clinic would need to get started with your case is the same information that you would need. I had a classmate that used a credit repair clinic. After working with them for a year, because of their fees, she still owed the exact amount of money that she owed when she started the previous year!

Consumer Debt:
Grab the Bull by the Horns!

How do I get started?

1.) The first step is to figure out your total income, the source of your income, and how often you receive this income (weekly, bi-weekly, monthly, or yearly).

Primary job

Part-time employment

Alimony

Child support

Rental property

Allowance

Dividends

Interest on investments, etc.

$ Total household income $

2.) The next step is to figure out who you owe and how much you owe them. The best place to start is with your credit report. Get a file cabinet, expandable file, a shoe box, or whatever works for you to start keeping track of your financial information.

3.) The third step is to start keeping up with and reading your bank statements, bills, and financial documents. Highlight all important information: interest rates, fees, payment due dates (some companies will change the due date and then charge you a late fee), etc., etc. Unbeknownst to me my credit card company changed my payment due date and then charged me $39.99 for paying late.

4.) The fourth step is to put credit cards away and stop creating new debt until you have your situation under control.

5.) Step five is to get a copy of your free credit report. Remember, go to: http://www.annualcreditreport.com.

6.) Step six is to take your time and review your report.

Look for and highlight information that may be inaccurate or incomplete. If you find errors, contact the credit bureau in writing to dispute the incorrect information. The credit bureau has 30 days to respond. You may want to dispute each item separately.

You should also contact the company, in writing, that gave the credit bureau the incorrect information. The telephone numbers and addresses of your creditors are located on your credit report. A dispute form should be available with your credit report. If a form is not available, you can send a dispute letter.

Locate receipts, canceled checks, or any other documents that may help prove your case. When dealing with the credit bureaus and your creditors, keep copies of all letters, forms, receipts, and documents that you send or receive. Be sure to keep a record of the names, dates, and arrangements that you make concerning your accounts. Do not trust other people to keep track of *your* information. It may be their job, but it is *your* life!

There is no need to stress if your credit score is low. My credit score was awful when I started on my journey, but with work and time, my score gradually started to increase. I am happy to reveal that I now have excellent credit! Once you gain control of your finances and reduce your debt, your score will begin to increase.

Do not become overwhelmed and give up. Relax and take your time. The end results will be worth the work.

Sample Dispute Letter

Date

Your Name
Your Address
Your City, State, Zip Code

Complaint Department
Name of Credit Reporting Agency
Address
City, State, Zip Code

Dear Sir or Madam:

I am writing to dispute the following information in my credit file. The item that I am disputing is highlighted on the attached photocopy of my credit report (identify item).

This item (name item) is (<u>inaccurate</u> or <u>incomplete)</u> because (state *why* it is inaccurate or incomplete). I am requesting that the item be (<u>deleted</u> or <u>corrected</u>).

Enclosed are copies of <u>documentation</u> (such as payment records or court documents) supporting my position. Please reinvestigate this matter and (<u>delete</u> or <u>correct</u>) the disputed item as soon as possible.

Sincerely,
Your name

Enclosures: (list information that you are enclosing)

Get Organized:
Prioritize and Write It Down!

After reviewing your credit report and taking charge of inaccurate information, the next step is to work on cleaning up your credit and reducing your debt. Trying mentally to keep up with your consumer debt and household expenses can be very confusing. Losing track of who has been paid and missing a payment, here or there, is understandable. The costs of such oversights, however, are late fees and higher interest rates.

It is time to get organized! Create an overview of your total financial responsibilities by combining your consumer debt and household expenses. Setting priorities for each of these items is important. When setting your priorities, keep in mind that there is a huge difference between a need and a want. We need shelter, electricity, heat, food, and water. We can survive without premium channels and special ring tones. Your willingness to sacrifice wants will depend on how badly you want to get out of debt. What is considered a need to one man may not be a need to another man, so set your priorities according to what is important to you and your family.

List all the names and remaining balances for each account, along with the interest rates. Also record the payment due dates for the accounts and the minimum payment required to keep your accounts in good standing.

I created my financial overview on the computer, but I enjoy writing information down the old-fashioned way. I purchased a $3.00 Home Finance and Bill Organizer from a dollar store. It works well for me. It is broken down by the month, and each month has its own pocket to hold my receipts and bills.

I simply fill in my financial information, and it allows me to keep track of my responsibilities for the month at a glance. If I need a receipt or financial statement, I just flip back to that month. It is also the perfect size if I want to drop it into my purse when I am out paying bills.

There is no perfect system: choose a system that works best for you. You can purchase computer software, a financial ledger, or a dollar theme book: the choice is yours.

Sample Financial Overview

<u>Household Expenses</u>:

Mortgage/Rent

Electricity

Heat

Water

Car Note

Medical Bills

Commuting Expenses

Groceries

Household Supplies (bath tissue, soap, toothpaste, etc.)

Homeowner's/Renter's Insurance

Property Tax

Home Security System

Life Insurance

Disability Insurance

Car Insurance

Cable

Home Telephone

Cell Phone

Child Support

Child Care

Time-share

Time-share Maintenance Fee

Consumer Debt:

Major Credit Card #1

Major Credit Card #2

Major Credit Card #3

Department Store Card #1

Department Store Card #2

Gas Card

Student Loan

Consumer Loan

<u>John Doe Finance and Debt Chart</u>

<u>Month:</u> _____

<u>Income:</u> _____

<u>Total Household Expenses:</u> _____

Account Name	Balance Payment	Amount Due	Due Date	Amount Paid

<u>Total Consumer Debt:</u> _____

Account Name	Balance	Interest Rate	Amount Due	Due Date	Amount Paid

Negotiating with Creditors

We have all heard the old saying that you can catch more flies with honey than with vinegar. When it comes to dealing with creditors, a spoonful of honey may not be such a bad idea. Creditors are probably tired of dealing with stressed and difficult people all day and would welcome a polite debtor. Do not give creditors a long sob story; instead, be polite, professional, and let them know that you are working to take charge of your debt and rebuild your credit.

When negotiating with your creditors, ask if they can reduce your interest rate or stop your interest from accruing, giving you the opportunity to get your debt under control. Be sure to speak with a supervisor or someone with the authority to make decisions. If they are not willing to negotiate, it is nothing personal; wait a week or two and try again. The worst thing that can happen is that they say no a second or third time; nothing lost, nothing gained. Be patient and consistent.

I know that most advisors suggest that you pay off the account with the highest interest rate first, but in my case I paid off the smallest accounts first. I had one account with a $3,500 balance and a high interest rate. I had another account with a balance of $500, but with a lower rate. It seemed to make more sense for me to pay off the account with the lower balance first and work my way up: the $500 account was within my reach. Once I paid that account in full, I applied the extra money to the next account. I continued with this formula until I was out of debt. I started with fourteen consumer debt accounts!

- Have a repayment plan that works best for your family. If one style does not work for you, try another one until it feels right.

- Know your budget before negotiating with creditors and never agree to pay more than you can afford; creditors will hold you to that amount.

- When negotiating, make sure to ask for a confirmation of the agreement in writing before sending money.

- Any information, which you send to creditors or collection agencies, send certified and request a receipt.

- Make a note of the person you are talking with during negotiations (name, date, and time of conversation).

- If the person you are dealing with is rude, end the call and call back another day; you are sure to deal with a different person.

- Your original creditor can turn your account over to a collection agency. Third-party debt collectors specialize in and get paid a fee or percentage for collecting unpaid debt.

- It is also common for different collection agencies to buy and sell your debt. Your original creditor may no longer be in the picture.

Chapter Two

You Can Afford to Save!

Finding Your
Wasted Wealth

"Knowing means nothing –
without doing."

Lucille Baldwin

Searching for Your
<u>Wasted Wealth</u>

Now that you have decided to take charge of your finances, it is time to find the extra money to begin eliminating your debt and reducing your expenses. This is where the real fun begins: trying to find out where your money is going. How many times have you asked yourself, "Where does my paycheck go every week?" "Why do I work so hard, but can never seem to make ends meet?" "What am I doing with my money?" If any of this seems familiar, you are not alone.

Living with debt can be extremely stressful. Believe me, if the head of the household is *STRESSED,* you can bet that stress will trickle down and affect the entire family. Speaking from personal experience, once you start taking charge of your finances, it will feel like imaginary weights being lifted from your shoulders. The next step on the journey is finding out where your money is going and working to remove those weights.

One of the best ways to find your wasted wealth is to start keeping track of your spending. I know that keeping track of your spending may seem tedious and time consuming. What I have learned, however, is that most of us waste more money than we realize, so shake off all the reasons for not doing it and just get started.

You do not need a lot to get started with this project; all you need is determination and a small notepad to jot down your purchases. If you do not like the idea of writing down your expenses as you go about your day, you can simply keep up with your receipts until you get home. A designated area in your wallet or an envelope will help you to keep up with your receipts. I suggest that you track your spending for at least a month. Yes, a month! I know that a month seems like a long time, but trust me, you can do it!

Target: "Budget Busters"

A $50.00
<u>Gallon of Milk</u>

I have to be honest, when I first started on my journey, I did not start with the previous suggestion. I was blindly feeling my way around and I was not sure in which direction I should go. Purely by chance, while cleaning out my miscellaneous drawer, I stumbled across a stack of old checkbooks. Flipping through my check stubs, I was surprised to discover that I was writing four to five checks a week at the supermarket.

I was spending hundreds of dollars a month purchasing small, unnecessary items. I would go into the supermarket to grab "a gallon of milk" and come out with $50 or more worth of items that I did not intend to buy.

The supermarket was not the only place that I was unknowingly wasting my money. I thought nothing of going to my local retail store and similar stores to browse, or to pick up one or two items. The problem was that I would, again, leave the store with merchandise that I had no intention of buying. Without realizing it, I was spending money that I should have set aside to pay bills. After going through months of old checkbooks, I discovered that I was blowing about $300 a month.

Finding that money was exciting and a real eye opener; I learned a valuable lesson. Now, before going to the store, I write down the items that I want to purchase or the amount that I am willing to spend. Sticking to a list was difficult at first, but with time, it became easier.

Impulse Buying:
A Wise Purchase or Money Wasted?

Do not fall for signs that read: for a limited time only, last day; maximum purchase: 6; or 4 boxes for $5.00. It is just a marketing trick to get you to spend money.

When we see signs with deadlines and signs that put limits on what we are allowed to purchase, it brings out the hoarder in us. It, also, jump-starts our survival instinct and we feel compelled to purchase those items before someone else beats us to it. The most alluring feature about impulse buying is price. If it is cheap enough, we will buy.

While out shopping I witnessed a relative give in to the urge to buy on impulse. She purchased 30 cans of discontinued cat food because the price was just too good to pass up; she saved a whopping 60% off the retail price. The only problem is that she does not have a cat! She rationalized the purchase by telling herself she would find someone who could use it. The urge to buy without thinking can be overwhelming. We pick up small items and toss them into our shopping cart, giving little thought to how they can add up over time.

Impulse buying is not limited to inexpensive items; with the availability of credit, it makes higher ticket purchasing more tempting. Buying makes us feel good, and buying with credit makes us feel better. It feels like getting free merchandise. When the price is more than we are willing to pay, however, we normally lose that good feeling. I think we have all, at one time or another, picked up an item and experienced sticker shock. This allows us to once again think clearly and we quickly put the item back. The best way to avoid impulse buying is to shop with a list. Always keep in mind that there is a difference between a need and a want when tempted to buy an item. You should step back and ask yourself, "Do I really need this item?" If the answer is no, then put it back on the shelf.

The Snack Machine:
Munching Your Way to the Poorhouse

The vending machine is the money monster in the room that fades into the background. Without noticing it, snack machines can easily gobble up your money. I would feed the machine at work a dollar for a sugary snack and a soda every morning. I would have a sweet roll with a drink mid-morning and purchase another snack by late afternoon, giving up another dollar. Everyone was doing this, so I thought nothing of it. My coworkers and I would sit around during our breaks laughing, talking, and enjoying this daily routine. The bad thing is that you buy a snack even if you are not hungry just because everyone else in the room is snacking. I spent another ten to twenty dollars a day going out to lunch with those same coworkers. What I was deducting from my wallet, I was adding to my waistline!

$12.00 a day for lunch and a snack (minimum)
x 5 days a week
$60.00 a week

$240.00 to $300.00 a month
or approximately
$3,120.00 a year!

As an alternative to eating lunch out and wasting money in the snack machines, I decided to do my wallet and waistline a favor. I started bringing my lunch from home, along with healthier snacks. The money that I saved was like receiving a raise and, to my surprise, I lost 30 pounds by eating healthier. Who knew healthy eating was good for you?

The ATM:
Easy Come, Easy Go

Another way that I caused chaos to my budget was depending on the automatic teller machine (ATM). There is something about the ATM that makes it feel like you are getting free money. There is also something very sexy and addictive about using an ATM. You insert your card, enter a few numbers, and clean, crisp bills magically appear. You feel important and special, and you are ready for a night out on the town. What could be better than that? Fun, friends, and *free cash*!

Having access to that cash is exhilarating. That is, until you find yourself short of money when it comes time to pay your bills. I was talking with Justin, a friend of mine, about using the ATM and how often he withdrew money. He admitted that, although he and his wife were having trouble making ends meet, he withdrew $20 each day on his way to work. He does not use the money to purchase exciting or whimsical items.

Instead, he uses the money, like most of us, to purchase a breakfast sandwich at a convenience store or from a fast-food restaurant on the way to work. Then he uses some of the money to purchase a mid-morning snack, and more fast food for lunch. The $20 that he withdraws each day during the week does not include the $50 in miscellaneous cash that he withdraws on the weekends. He admits that he cannot afford to waste the money that he withdraws from the ATM each day, but it has become a nasty habit.

$20.00 a day (ATM)
x 5 days a week
$100.00 a week

Withdrawing twenty dollars here or there may not seem like much money, but it is easy to lose track and spend more than you can afford. That twenty dollars a day could easily help Justin eliminate a bill. He could help his budget by eating breakfast at home and bringing his own snacks, then he could reduce his withdrawals to $10 a day, saving $50 a week.

I stood in Justin's shoes, withdrawing money from the ATM to purchase small, unimportant items, not realizing the harm that I was doing to my financial stability. Once I understood how much money I was randomly taking out of my account, I stopped using the ATM. I also decided to cancel my PIN number to remove the temptation. Without access to the automatic teller machine, I was no longer able to withdraw money at a whim, and was forced to depend on planning. The benefit: less unplanned spending and more money in my account.

Shopping as a Form of Entertainment

At an early age, we learn that one of the greatest places to hang out is the mall. As we walk around and browse with our favorite people, we cannot wait to start spending money. The magic starts the moment we walk through the front doors with all of our senses stimulated. The beautiful displays, a hint of perfume in the air, the smell of freshly baked cookies, soft music, and children laughing relaxes us and we feel welcomed. A great deal of research and money go into finding the best ways to separate us from our money, and it is obviously working. Think about it: where else other than the mall are we willing to pay $5.00 for a 35-cent cookie?

Depending on the mall and stores for fun or simply out of boredom is a good way to stay in debt. Until you get your debt and willpower under control, hanging out at stores is detrimental to your finances.

Try to come up with other forms of entertainment that do not include looking for items to purchase. Enjoying family and friends while playing board games can be an alternative to cruising the stores. Convincing ourselves to spend money is easy. Convincing ourselves to get out of debt takes work.

Peer Pressure – Adult Style
(Keeping Up with the Joneses)

The pressure to fit in can create a lot of debt. When we leave school, we pack away our yearbooks, leave behind the popular kids, the jocks, and the bullies. We leave behind the stress of wearing the perfect outfits and fitting in with the right crowd. On that special day we toss our caps into the air and leave behind classmates, bad skin, and peer pressure. Right? Not always.

Peer pressure can only follow us into our adult lives if we feel the need to keep up with our neighbors and coworkers. We give in to peer pressure if we constantly agree to hang out with friends over dinner and drinks when our budget is tight. We give in to peer pressure when we live in homes that are beyond our means and drive cars that we struggle to pay for. We give in to peer pressure every time we max out our credit cards to pay for vacations and the perfect outfits.

Chances are, the people that you are trying to impress are up to their necks in debt trying to impress you. The sad thing is that we live in a world where people are literally starving to death, have no clean water to drink, and are sleeping on dirt floors. If our biggest concern is being seen in the same outfit twice, or driving a car that is reliable but old, then we should consider ourselves lucky. We live in a great country where we have the power to control our destiny.

When we realize that we are more than the sum of our possessions, we can start to make a change. People will only have power over you if you give it to them. You do not have to create debt to fit in with real friends — or anyone for that matter. Your neighbors and coworkers will respect you for doing what they do not have the courage to do. Do not envy the Joneses. The Joneses have their own problems.

A Mailbox Full of Bills and a
Home Full of Things

We get hooked on buying things: things for the house, things for the car, things for the kids. We want to have more things than our coworkers and better things than our neighbors. We judge people and ourselves on the number of things that we own. But, a closet full of must-have things or a garage full of fancy things will do little for you in a financial emergency.

Not only do we buy things, but we also collect things. I was watching a television program where a woman in her sixties was about to lose her home. Her house was in foreclosure, and she was weeks away from being forced to move out.

What I noticed about her home was that she had snow globes everywhere. She had snow globes on special shelves that she had built. She had snow globes on end tables and snow globes covering the coffee table. She even had snow globes in her kitchen and bathroom. Collecting snow globes was her passion.

What crossed my mind while watching the show was that her passion for collecting snow globes could not help her financially. I must admit that I had a collection of dolls that were of very little financial value. I had no savings, no emergency account, and no financial education, but I had a doll collection. Because of my financial ignorance, I purchased many of the dolls using my credit card. So, not only was I wasting money on dolls that depreciated, but I was also paying more than 20% in interest for them.

We get hooked on collecting for a variety of reasons. In my case, I always wanted a room full of dolls when I was a little girl. I foolishly thought because I was a working adult, I could afford to collect dolls; I was wrong. Collecting items can be a lot of fun, but cannot replace an emergency fund, retirement account, or benefit you in your time of financial need.

Collecting items that depreciate is another way that we waste money. Just consider that collectibles overall do not make great investments. Collect for enjoyment, if you can also afford to fund your emergency account and save for your retirement.

DVDs: Your Personal Movie Library

I love a good movie as much as the next person, but the money that I see people spending to build a movie library is crazy. Most new releases in my area are $19.99 each, plus tax. Unless it is a movie that you and your family love and will watch repeatedly, save your money.

The Internet offers movies and television shows twenty-four hours a day, or you can rent a movie in some places for as little as $1.00. Do not get caught up in the personal movie library phase; instead, use that money to benefit you and your family.

The Gym:
<u>Death Before Cancellation</u>

Have you ever tried to cancel a gym membership? Good luck. I tried to cancel my membership because I was taking charge of my finances. I was told that I could end my memberships in one of two ways: if I could prove that I was moving out of the state or dead. Since I signed a contract, I was obligated to pay the $50.00 a month membership fee until my contract was over. Be sure that a gym membership is something that you are ready to commit to before signing a contract.

Cell Phones: The Hidden Cost

With so many options available, how much can you really afford to pay for your cell phone? There are camera phones, phones with access to the Internet, phones with the ability to download ring tones, and phones that allow you to play your favorite games. I hear people talking about their cell-phone bills all the time. It is shocking how much money is being spent for the convenience of owning a cell phone. I received a call from a major telephone service provider recently. They offered me 300 free daytime minutes per month to sign with their company. But 300 free daytime minutes only averages out to 10 minutes a day. The cost for going over my "free" minutes would be 29 cents a minute. Ouch!

It is not unusual for people to pay hundreds of dollars a month because of roaming fees or going over their available minutes. William, one of my best friends, paid $369 one month and $429 the next month because of roaming fees. I met another lady, Pat, who paid $1,000 one month to talk with her boyfriend who moved to another state. A cell phone can destroy your budget if you are not careful. Only pay for what you need or can afford. Do you need access to the Internet? Do you really need a camera phone? Do you need to pay for special ring tones when an old-fashioned ring will do? My only question is, "What the heck is everyone talking about?"

The Lottery: Chasing a Dream...
<u>The Odds Are Against You!</u>

Chasing the American dream for some of us may start with the purchase of a lottery ticket. Do not fool yourself into believing that your only chance for achieving a better life is through gambling. Spending your money on lottery tickets is not the path to financial freedom. Purchasing tickets occasionally for fun is one thing; purchasing tickets on a regular basis in hope of changing your life is another.

Studies consistently show that the people least able to afford to purchase lottery tickets are the ones funding the millions of dollars in lottery revenue. The truth is that 20% of the people purchasing lottery tickets are funding about 80% of the revenue.

After the 20% have created huge jackpots, the more affluent crowd is now willing to purchase a lottery ticket. They are willing to spend a few dollars to take a chance on jackpots that are now worth millions.

While the 20% are building the jackpots, those who know better than to *invest* in lottery tickets are paying their bills and investing in their future. Instead of purchasing lottery tickets, use that money to get out of debt. Instead of wasting your money, learn to create and fund your own big payday.

FYI: Even if you win the jackpot, studies reveal that up to 80% of lottery winners will lose their winnings in about five years.

To Lend or Not to Lend?
That is the Question

William Shakespeare's Polonius said it best when giving advice to his son, Laertes, in *Hamlet*: *"Neither a borrower nor a lender be; for loan oft loses both itself and friend..."*

To put it simply: The fastest way to lose both your money and a friend is to borrow or lend money. I have lent money in the past, and it is not worth losing friends or the strain that it can put on relationships. There is an uneasiness in the air when someone owes you money. Before long, you start to notice everything that they buy: a new outfit, a vehicle, or a simple cup of coffee. You may begin to resent their spending habits.

You think to yourself that they could have paid off, or at least paid on, their debt with the money they are spending. It should go without saying that my answer to the question, to lend or not to lend, is not to lend! I am more than willing to help find a solution, but no longer with financial assistance.

Thinking of saying no to a family member or friend in their time of need can be stressful. If you do consider giving a loan, it should be an amount of money that you can afford to give as a gift, in case the loan is not repaid. You should never lend money you need for your own living expenses or money that you depend on for emergencies. Consider what is best for your family and financial situation.

When Friends or Family Move In

Your brother, a best friend from college, or your kids may need a place to stay "just until they can get themselves together." How do you decide whether or not to allow friends or family to move in with you? After all, your home is your safe haven, a place to get away from the stresses of everyday life.

The problem is that people are not always as appreciative once they have your cash or keys to the front door. Your houseguest may not feel the need to help with chores or contribute to the everyday running of the house. He (she) may consider himself a houseguest and expect you to provide necessities such as food, drinks, and toiletry items. Coming home to a messy house and an increase in your utilities can put a strain on the best relationships.

Choosing to open your home when someone is going through a tough time is a difficult decision, but consider that a month on your sofa can easily turn into a year.

"It's No Big Deal —
It's Only $1.00"

How many times have you looked at your bank fees or bank statement and thought to yourself, "It is no big deal — it is only a dollar"? A dollar may not seem like a lot of money to you, but it adds up to a nice sum of money for financial institutions. Instead of going to the banks, that money should be adding up in your account.

Remember the old saying "laughing all the way to the bank"? The laughter these days is coming from inside the bank. A large percentage of profit for many banks is from fees that they charge to their customers. Since you and I are their customers, we are making a lot of other people rich.

In one year, the banking industry can make over 50 billion dollars in fees. That is a lot of cabbage, a lot of dinero, dough, or bread; any way you slice it, it is too much money to give up without thought. Take charge of your money, or other people will gladly take it from you.

One of the ways that banks earn so much money is that we give them the power to take advantage of our mistakes. I have bounced a couple of checks myself, and I had no one to blame but myself. Writing checks and not keeping track of my spending, writing checks before I put the money in the bank, etc., etc. . . . There are so many ways that you can screw up your bank accounts. The biggest mistake is not taking charge and losing track of your money.

Fees, Fees, and More Fees

One major way that banks earn money is from the non-sufficient funds (NSFs) category, also known as an overdraft. If you have ever received a notice from your bank informing you that you had a check returned for NSFs, fees and more fees may be all you can think about. You may mumble a few not-so-nice words to yourself. Your next step, however, should be to figure out how many more checks may still be floating around, waiting to hit your checking account.

If you are new to the check writing or debit card arena, trust the rest of us, an overdraft or returned check notice is not something that you want to find in your mailbox.

Overdraft Fees

What is an overdraft?

An overdraft happens when you have *less* money in your bank account than you are trying to spend.

What can cause an overdraft?

An overdraft can occur when you lose track of your spending. With all the technology available to withdraw money from your bank account today, it is very easy, but *costly* to forget to write down a transaction or two.

What are some of the ways to withdraw money from my account?

- Writing a <u>check</u>

- Using your bank-issued <u>debit card</u> to make purchases

- Using the <u>ATM</u> (<u>A</u>utomatic <u>T</u>eller <u>M</u>achine) to get cash

- Setting up an <u>automatic</u> bill <u>payment</u>

- Making an <u>electronic payment</u> (over the telephone or Internet).

What happens if I spend more than I have in my account?

If you make a mistake and spend more than you have in your account, your bank, credit union, or savings and loan can choose either to pay the amount or not to pay the amount for you.

If you do not have the money in your account and they

choose to pay the amount for you, you will be charged an "*overdraft*" fee by your bank.

What is an overdraft fee?

An overdraft fee is the amount that your bank charges for covering your promise to vendors when you fall short or make a mistake with your account. This act of kindness on the part of the bank may cost you around $30.00 <u>per transaction</u>.

What happens if they do not pay?

This is when it can really become costly for you. If they choose not to pay the amount for you and *return the check*, they will charge you a "returned check" fee or "non-sufficient funds" fee. Not only will you owe your bank a fee, but you will also owe a returned check fee to the company or business where you wrote the check.

That means that you will need to cover the cost of the check, the bank fee, plus the fee charged by the company or business where you wrote the check. The fees that companies and businesses charge may also run about $30.00.

A $20.00 returned check can easily cost you $80.00 or more.

> $20.00 amount of check
>
> $30.00 bank fee
>
> + $30.00 fee to business or company
>
> $80.00 (that's only one transaction)

Remember that overdraft fees and returned check fees are for *each* transaction or check, and the companies may repeatedly present the check to the bank to collect their money, resulting in more fees for each transaction.

What should I do if I have an overdraft or returned check?

Try to make a deposit into your account as soon as possible, to cover the total amount. You will also need to cover any fees and charges added to your account. If you still have transactions and checks due to hit your account, you will need to deposit enough money to cover those transactions. You can also talk with your customer service representative at the bank for suggestions on the best way to handle the situation.

What is the best way to avoid bank fees?

The best and least expensive way to avoid bank fees is to stay on top of your checking account. Mistakes happen, but keeping track of your transactions is the best way to cut down on the chance that you will bounce a check or suffer an overdraft fee.

It may feel like an inconvenience to write down every transaction. In the end, however, it can save you a great deal of time and money.

- Review your bank statement.

- Keep your receipts and write down your ATM withdrawals.

- Keep track of your automatic and electronic payments.

- Know how much money you have in your account.

- Keep track when you use your debit card.

- Respect your money and your money will respect you.

Another way to cover yourself is to have overdraft protection.

What is overdraft protection?

For a fee, most banks offer a plan to help keep costs down from overdrafts and returned checks. A protection plan will allow your ATM and debit card transactions to go through and prevent your checks from being returned when your account is short.

Keep in mind that banks are in the business of making money, so this is *not a free service*. Your bank, credit union, or savings and loan company will charge you a fee for *each* check or overdraft transaction.

The benefit of the plan is that you will avoid the returned check fee to the company or business where you wrote the check, and not turning up on a bad check writers' list can save you a great deal of embarrassment.

What is the cost of an overdraft protection plan?

The cost and benefits of overdraft protection plans may vary with each bank, savings and loan company, or credit union. They may also set a limit on the amount of money your account may be overdrawn.

It is a good idea to shop around for a financial institution to find the one whose services best fit your needs. Talk to customer service representatives at different banks to find out what services they offer and the fees they charge.

Are there any other ways to cover overdrafts?

Some banks allow you to link your savings account to your checking account. If you should overdraw your checking account, they can take the money from your savings account to cover the check or transaction.

Some banks also offer a loan in the form of a "line of credit." This works like a regular loan and requires good credit. If you should go over your account balance, the bank will *lend* you the money to cover the check or overdraft. Fees and interest apply.

The Best Laid Plans

It is not a good idea to depend on the different protection plans and services to cover checks and transactions. There is no 100% guarantee that your bank, credit union, or savings and loan company will cover the many transactions that can overdraw your account. It is a lot easier to prevent an overdraft or returned check than it is to clean up the mess of creating them.

As I stated earlier, the best and least expensive way to avoid fees is to stay on top of your accounts. Take the time to write down your transactions and checks, and keep track of the automatic payments that you have set up. Balance your checkbook, and take the time to know what is going on with your money.

The High to Low

of

Check Processing

A bit of interesting information is that some banks, as a "courtesy" to us (*wink*), start processing the largest checks first from our account. The banks do this so that more important checks have a better chance of clearing our account in case of a mistake or overdraft.

The theory is that higher dollar amount checks are more likely checks for a mortgage payment, car payment, or insurance, and that it is more important to clear those checks than a smaller dollar amount to a shoe store.

The Theory

You have $400.00 in your checking account, and the bank receives four of your checks on the same day:

> $ 55.00 Dry Cleaning
>
> $ 75.00 Shoe Store
>
> $100.00 Restaurant
>
> $350.00 Life Insurance

In this case the bank would put through your life insurance check first, and the other three less-important checks would not clear. Using this system seems fair because who wants their life insurance to be cancelled? Using the high-to-low process will create three checks being returned instead of just one.

$400.00 Balance in Checking Account

- $350.00 Check for Life Insurance

$ 50.00 ***New Checking Account Balance***

- $100.00 Check for Restaurant (NSFs)

- $ 75.00 Check for Shoe Store (NSFs)

- $ 55.00 Check for Dry Cleaning (NSFs)

Same Theory:

You still have $400.00 in your checking account, and the bank receives four of your checks on the same day in the following order:

$50.00 water bill, $75.00 life insurance, $100.00 car insurance, and $350.00 leather jacket.

$400.00 Balance in Checking Account

- $350.00 Check for Leather Jacket (Great Sale)

$ 50.00 ***New Checking Account Balance***

- $100.00 Check for Car Insurance (NSF)

- $ 75.00 Check for Life Insurance (NSF)

- $ 50.00 Check for Water Bill (NSF)

Under the high-to-low theory, you will still have three checks that you will generate fees from, three important checks that will go unpaid. If the bank had processed your checks in the order that they received them, only one check would have been returned for NSFs.

The Reloadable or Prepaid Card:
Interest Free, but "Loaded with Fees"

A few years ago, while standing in line at a well-known retail chain, I noticed an application for a reloadable credit card. What a great idea, I thought to myself, a reloadable credit card would be perfect for my daughter, who had recently started college. I could load the card from my end, and my daughter could purchase the items that she needs while she is away from home.

Since one of the most important lessons that I learned was to start reading the fine print, I read that there was a fee to activate the card, and a monthly fee deducted to maintain the card. I decided that the reloadable card was not the best choice for my needs.

What is a reloadable or prepaid credit card?

A reloadable or prepaid card looks like your credit or debit card. The difference between a prepaid card and a credit card is that you are limited by money you load on your card. The big draw to the reloadable and prepaid cards is that, unlike credit cards, there is no interest charged for using these products.

In place of interest charges, however, they charge "fees." There are many plans available when it comes to reloadable and prepaid cards. It is up to you to research which plan, if any, works best for you and your family. I came across a list of charges and fees that may interest you:

- Annual fee $0.00 - $39.95

- Activation fee $0.00 - $29.95

- Monthly fee $2.00 - $9.95

- Reload fee $2.00 - $9.95 (a fee to add money to your account)

- Maintenance fee $4.95/month or $1.00 per transaction up to $10.00 a month

- Transaction fee $0.00 - $10.00 (a fee to spend your money)

- Inactivity fee $1.95 month (after 90 days of inactivity)

- Request a statement fee $0.00 - $5.00 (mailed statement)

- Purchases using your PIN number $1.00 (US)

- Purchases using your signature $1.00 (US)

- ATM inquiry fee (US) $0.00 - $5.00

- ATM cash withdrawal $2.00 (in addition to any bank fees)

- Customer service fee $0.00 - $5.00 (to speak with a live representative)

- Customer service fee $0.00 - $2.00 (automated calls)

You work hard for your money and deserve to keep as much as possible. I can tell you from personal experience and from observing the spending habits of people that a great deal of money passes through our hands. You may not believe it, but if you have faith in the process and take the time to search, you *will* find your wasted wealth. People often tell me that they know they should start taking charge of their finances, but *knowing means nothing, without doing.*

Chapter Three

A Loyal Employee:

<u>Putting Your Found</u>
<u>Money to Work</u>

*"Do not be shocked by a loss of income;
be prepared."*

Lucille Baldwin

"Pay Yourself First"
<u>You Deserve It!</u>

I am not a morning person, and I absolutely hate getting up early. It is sometimes dark, wet, or cold outside when the alarm clock goes off: the signal for us to rise and shine whether we want to or not. We all have different routines for getting out of bed. Some of us will hit the snooze button several times. Some of us will pull a pillow or blanket over our heads to gain one extra minute of sleep. Others, like my daughter, will jump up with the first ring. Getting up and going to work every day should be enough to earn the top spot in the payment line. Still, for some reason the thought of paying ourselves does not occur to us. So, what makes us worthy of being paid first, especially ahead of bill collectors?

Have you ever been stuck in traffic on a really hot day and watched construction workers through your window? Wondering to yourself, "How can they work so hard outside in what must feel like an oven?" I have, and when I think back to those moments, I realize that they are worthy.

Do you shop on holidays? If you do, then you must realize that retail workers make it possible by sacrificing that day with their own families, and that they are worthy. If you get up an hour early so that you can take your kids to school on your way to work, then you are worthy. If you have ever waved down a taxicab driver or depended on a police officer for help, then you know that they are worthy. If you stand on your feet all day at work and take classes at night, then you are worthy. If you put on a uniform, heels, or a shirt and tie before going to work, then you are worthy. If you teach our children or serve our country, then you, too, are worthy, and you deserve to be paid first. *We are everyday people, doing everyday jobs. We are worthy, and we deserve it!*

Taking charge of your finances and paying yourself will give you the power to control your future. Always keep in mind that your income level is not as important as what you do with your money. A person earning $20,000 a year can be better off financially than a person earning $50,000, if that $50,000 earner is not in control of his or her income. Once you take charge of your spending, you will be surprised, no, you will be *amazed*, by the amount of extra money that you will be able to save and invest.

Preparing for a Storm
<u>While the Sun is Shining</u>

A storm is a *violent disturbance of the atmosphere,* with strong winds and usually rain, thunder, lightning, or snow. If you know the above definition to be true, then you know that the time to prepare for a storm is not after the winds, rain, or thunder has started. It can be stressful and frightening to wait until a storm has begun to seek shelter; the same can be said when going through a financial storm. Waiting until you are in the midst of financial chaos to act cannot be the plan.

A Small Emergency Fund for
<u>Everyday Living</u>

Now that you have found your wasted wealth and you realize that you deserve to pay yourself first, it is time to start putting that money to good use. The goal of preparing for emergencies is to reduce your dependency on others, and to take charge of your own financial responsibilities. Even if you are up to your neck in bills, it is important to work on building your emergency fund. Unexpected expenses will not wait until you are out of debt to show up.

You may be wondering how much money you will need in your account. That answer will depend entirely on your situation, and what *you* consider small emergencies. Think back and remind yourself how much small, unexpected emergencies have cost you in the past. Was it three hundred dollars? Eight hundred dollars? Was it necessary to borrow money or to turn to your credit cards to handle the problem?

Everyday occurrences happen every day. You have two choices: you can either prepare ahead of time, or you can simply deal with the aftermath. Choosing the latter will normally make the situation worse. If you own a vehicle, replacing the tires or paying for repairs will be necessary. Those repairs can easily cost hundreds of dollars. The reality is that eventually all vehicles will need some type of repair work, or just basic maintenance, to keep them running smoothly.

Repair work on your vehicle is not the only emergency that can send you running for your credit cards or to a loan company to borrow money. Because of normal wear and tear, roofs leak and hot water heaters and other appliances may require maintenance or replacement. Are you buying or renting your home? Renters are usually not responsible for normal wear and tear; they can simply call the homeowner or property manager to handle the situation. Allowing for that fact, if you are a homeowner, buying your home, or own rental property, you may need more money in your fund than a renter. While renting, I found that *maintaining* $1,000 in my fund was sufficient to keep my household running smoothly. It was enough to cover car repairs and small issues.

Life happens. Sometimes due to an illness, injury, or death unplanned trips or unexpected bills may pop up. Suppose you have a sick child, and she needs you to stay home to take care of her? What would you do? There is nothing worse than leaving a sick child, or sending that sick child to school, because *you cannot afford* to miss a day or two of work. I have been there and done that and, believe me, it is a feeling of guilt that you will not forget.

I have no problem telling you that I started my fund with 25 cents! I got a jar and started consistently feeding it quarters. To speed up the process, whenever I went to the bank I would buy a roll of quarters, and before long, I saved enough money to fund my account. The main rule for using the account was that I had to replace anything that I withdrew as soon as possible. By replacing the funds, I would be prepared for the next unplanned expense, and I could continue to borrow money from myself, *interest free*. I learned to become a very strict lender, making myself repay the money within weeks instead of months. This meant that before I purchased a new outfit, ate out, or bought any unnecessary items, I had to "repay each loan."

Another rule was that the money could only be withdrawn for *real* emergencies. My cravings for jumbo shrimp and snow crab legs did not qualify as an emergency, nor did a night out on the town with friends, nor a new pair of shoes.

Because money is tight, you may not believe that you can afford to start saving. The truth: If money is tight, you can't afford *not* to start saving!

A Major Emergency Fund:
<u>Preparing for the "Expected"</u>

Building a major emergency fund is extremely important in case of a job loss, illness, or any situation that interrupts your income or drastically increases your expenses. A loss of income will not put a stop to your mortgage payment, car note, or other financial responsibilities.

What if you had the power to look into a crystal ball and it revealed that your company was planning to lay you off within the next six months? What if you also learned that it would take you months to find another job? How would you choose to spend your remaining paychecks? Would you continue to create debt and purchase unnecessary items, or would you start planning for those months when you would be without an income?

Three weeks after Christmas at an employee meeting, the company that I worked for gave me the opportunity to peek into that crystal ball. That morning, the store manager informed us that eight of my coworkers were being terminated, *effective immediately*. After years of service, they were fired without warning. They walked through the front door that morning with a full-time job and benefits, and walked out two hours later with neither.

The manager also informed us that they could return in two weeks, and the company would be willing to rehire them as part-time employees, *without benefits:* no medical, dental, or vision insurance; no paid vacations; no 401(k); no sick or personal leave; no disability or life insurance. Other managers were holding similar meetings throughout the organization, affecting thousands of workers. It was a win-win situation for the company; they rehired returning workers with experience, while saving money because of the elimination of their benefits.

When the employees of one of my favorite restaurants went to work one morning, they found a sign with chains and locks hanging from the front door. The sign stated that the restaurant was "closed." Again, the job losses came without warning! Can you imagine the hurt and fear of going to work one day and finding the doors locked? Imagine the fear if you are living paycheck to paycheck. Through friends and coworkers I realized that without a plan, I was clearly viewing my future. To avoid a similar fate, it was time for me to rethink my life and take a different path.

We will rarely have the luxury of being warned about a loss of income. We can only learn from the past and the experiences of others that the possibility is all too real and then prepare. Again, life happens. Prepare for "expected" situations.

Start Building Your Funds
(A Penny, Quarter, or Dollar at a Time)

Most financial advisors suggest having three to twelve months of living expenses in your emergency fund. With many companies closing and the growing number of jobs lost, I like the idea of a twelve-month cushion. I know that twelve months, even three months, may seem like a lot when you are trying to make ends meet, but it is possible with a plan.

The key to building your fund is to not focus on the big picture. Instead, think of it as a math problem, and break it down to its simplest form. If you do not have an emergency fund, the first step is to open two savings accounts: one for small emergencies and another for major emergencies. I love my credit union because I was able to open both accounts for only five dollars each.

So, no more excuses claiming that money is too tight. If you can only afford to pay yourself a quarter, then pay yourself a quarter. I do not care if you can only afford a penny; then pay yourself a penny. The key to your success will be to keep paying yourself until your pennies or quarters become dollars. During a trip to Atlantic City with my family, I noticed that many of the casinos had areas lined with penny slot machines. Looking at all those machines only reinforced my belief that pennies can also create wealth, if you have enough of them! This does not mean that it is okay to run out and gamble; it means that no amount is too small to start paying yourself. *(My mother continues to insist that she was not gambling at the casinos; she was just "playing the machines.")*

When you begin building your fund, remember to set a goal that is within your reach. I never used to set goals for myself in the past. I just allowed life to happen, and *then* I reacted. When I set goals for myself now, I always take out a piece of paper and draw a ladder. I visualize myself standing at the foot of that ladder and I write down my goal at the top. Then on each rung, I write down the steps that I need to take to reach the top. Finally, I picture myself climbing that ladder one step at a time, just like Jack climbing the beanstalk.

Your Christmas Debt:
Leaving It Behind

Christmas is a day that can create unnecessary debt. The one thing about Christmas that we can always count on is that it falls on the same date each year, giving us three hundred and sixty-five days to prepare. The insanity is that we are somehow caught off guard every year, and we sing the same "I cannot believe the holidays are here already" song.

Take the stress out of the holidays by planning early. Most banks, credit unions, and other financial institutions offer Christmas club accounts. If you celebrate the holidays, then you know that day is coming. Do yourself and your credit cards a favor, and prepare for the holidays ahead of time. Do not wait until the first of December to try to figure out how you are going to pay for gifts, and then turn to credit cards or loans.

By planning ahead, you can leave your Christmas debt behind you and not drag bills into the New Year. If you cannot afford to shop for the holidays, do not give in to pressure, or allow anyone to make you feel guilty. The people that really love you do not care about gifts. Send them your love or spend quality time with them. This should also include birthdays and other special days. Do not create debt just for one day!

The Perfect Day

My Dream Wedding

With this ring I thee wed; and with this credit card, in the name of love, I pledge to create debt. We do not plan to start our new life with the person that we love over our heads in debt. On average, however, American couples spend about $28,000 for their wedding and another $1,000 for the dress. The nearly $30,000 price tag does not even include the cost of the honeymoon or the engagement ring. The ring can add another $3,200 with the honeymoon adding $5,000. Studies reveal that the number-one reason couples argue is because of money, which can eventually lead to *divorce*. Which is more important: a wedding that you cannot afford or spending your life with the one you love?

Most engaged couples spend 50% more on their wedding than they planned, usually creating debt. The reality is that your financial responsibilities will be around long after your dream day has ended. I have often heard people say that they have been dreaming of their wedding day for years. Well, unless you come from a wealthy family or you have a nice bank account, the day you start dreaming is the day you should start saving.

<u>My Wedding Planning Promises...</u>

My dream day will not dip into my parents' retirement fund.

My dream day will not create years of credit card debt.

My dream day will not take away from my financial security.

My dream day will not become a financial burden for others.

My dream day will not exceed our budget.

My dream day debt will not outlast our love...

Parents, Dear Parents:
<u>Who is Going to Pay for *Their* Dream Day?</u>

When we have children, we want to give them the world and place it at their feet. No matter how old they are, in our eyes, they will always be our babies depending on us to provide their needs. We cannot, however, spend money that we do not have or create debt to cater to their wants. If you can afford it and are willing to pay for your child's dream day, go for it.

If, on the other hand, you do not have the resources to pay for your adult children to have their dream day, saying no is okay. Do not allow your adult children to pressure you into paying for an expensive wedding that you cannot afford. We do not owe our children an expensive wedding. Unless you can write a check without creating debt or dipping into your retirement account or emergency funds, they should pay for their own wedding. Why should you pay $30,000 for a wedding if you still have a mortgage, credit card debt, and no savings?

Prepare for Retirement Today
or
<u>Live in Poverty Tomorrow</u>

With the passing of each day, we are a day closer to retirement. Most people are not planning for retirement, because they are under the false assumption that their Social Security benefits will be enough to support them. Although these benefits do provide *some income* during retirement, they were *never* meant to be the only source.

Because of a lack of knowledge and naive assumptions, Social Security has unfortunately become the main source of income for almost 50% of retirees. In reality, your monthly check will only replace about 40% of your earnings, and alone may not even provide a standard of living above the poverty line. Nevertheless, according to the US Department of Health & Human Services, 96% of all Americans will retire financially dependent on the government, family, or charity.

Social Security was meant to be a boost to your retirement savings and cannot replace a sound financial plan. Most financial advisors state that you will need 75% or more annually of your current income to live comfortably in retirement; 90% or more if you are in a lower income bracket. Instead of spending money without thought, it is time to start preparing for your future. Your Social Security benefits, along with insurance, savings, a pension, and investments, will make for a more comfortable retirement. For full details about Social Security, go to the official government website, Government Made Easy, at www.usa.gov. Search: Social Security.

Hey!
What Happened to
My F*/$#@! Pension?

To achieve "the American retirement dream," we were taught to work hard and remain loyal to our employers. In return, they would reward us with a fair pension during our twilight years. For some of us, that dream may turn into a nightmare once we realize this: not only is Social Security not meant as a main source of income, but also our private pensions may not be what we expected. The reality about private pensions, according to Cyril Brickfield, the former director of American Association of Retired People (AARP), is that "private pensions are in a state of chaos."

- Fifty (50) percent of the workforce today has *no* pension.

- Thirty-seven (37) percent have ineffective pensions that pay between $55 to $300 a month.

I learned that after more than twenty years of service, I fall into the ineffective pension range. Imagine my surprise when I received my retirement package, informing me that at retirement age I would receive a monthly pension check of $81.02 — a whopping $972.24 a year! They also informed me that if I chose to receive my money before the age of sixty-seven, I would receive even less. I am about twenty-five years away from retirement age. Can you imagine what $81.02 will be worth in twenty-five years? Perhaps a gallon of milk.

I decided to return to my former place of employment and share this information with my ex-coworkers. This was not the type of news that you should receive in the mail, months before retiring. If they were armed with this information now, they would still have time to take charge of their retirement and come up with a plan. The employees that had already retired never came back and told us how little we could expect; we never thought to check. We all *assumed* that we would receive a nice pension after retirement.

I did not tell them how much I would be receiving. Instead, I wanted them to guess how much they thought I would receive each month. Most of them started at $1,000 per month and s-l-o-w-l-y worked their way down. I could see the shock in their faces when they got down to $300, and I was still telling them, "No."

After sharing my information, a few people decided to check on their own retirement packages. On average, they found out that after thirty years with the company they would be receiving about $231 a month. That means that they will have a pension income of about $2,772 a year! All I can say: Welcome to the real world.

Retirement:
The Consequences of Not Preparing
(The Choice Is Yours)

According to the Social Security Administration, if you randomly take 100 people at the start of their working careers and follow them for 40 years, at retirement age:

1 will be wealthy,

4 will be financially secure,

5 will continue working out of need,

36 will be dead,

and

54 will be <u>dead</u> <u>broke</u>...

depending on their Social Security checks, family, and even charity. If you are left to tell the story, where will you fall?

Money for Retirement:
Pensions, Savings, and Benefits

Because of financial ignorance, I got off to a late start with my own retirement savings. Growing up with the false assumption that my Social Security benefits and pension would see me through retirement, I never gave much thought to planning for the future. I went to work every day, paid my taxes, was loyal to my company, and assumed that my future was set. Once I started taking charge of my finances, however, I was hit, kicked, and slapped in the face with reality. I realized that I had better get serious about my retirement.

Like others around me, I always assumed you had to have a lot of money to invest. I grew up believing that old saying, "It takes money, to make money." I have learned many lessons on my journey, and cleared up many false assumptions. I think three of the most important lessons that I learned were to:

keep my debt low,

spend less than I earn,

and pay myself on a regular basis.

These are lessons that anyone can learn. Life would be easier if we learned and followed such simple rules at an early age.

Since I am not in the banking business, a financial advisor, or an accountant, I will not be dispensing professional financial advice. I can only continue to share information and challenges that have crossed my path. Once I had control of my finances and eliminated my debt, I felt it was time to branch out and move beyond the basic savings account.

You may want to consider eliminating your debt before you

begin investing your money. It did not make sense for me to earn 4% interest on an investment, while I was paying 24% interest and more on my credit cards and loans. By paying off my debt first, I was able to save thousands of dollars in interest and fees. Instead of making monthly payments to credit card companies and other financial institutions, I was able to use that money to start investing. I decided to start at places where I felt comfortable, asking questions at my credit union, other banks, and my insurance company.

When it comes to investing and risk-taking, we all have different levels of comfort. To say that I am extremely conservative when it comes to investing money would be an enormous understatement. Taking a chance on losing money is not in my makeup. When I do go to casinos (I have family in Atlantic City), I take $20 and a book. If I do not hit the jackpot with $20 or less, then I know it was not meant to be. I have friends who are a little more daring than I am; I watched one of them lose up to 80% of his investments. Do your research; speak with a financial planner, and only do what makes you comfortable.

Because I am so conservative, I do not mind earning less money if I know that my money is somewhere safe. My goal is to pay as little in interest and fees to others as possible, and to use *that money* to invest and purchase items that will benefit me when I retire. So, instead of making a monthly payment to a credit card company, I can purchase a bond every month. Instead of having a car note, I can add money to my IRA account. Instead of repaying a loan at 24% interest, I can use the money to purchase certificates of deposit. Instead of making a weekly payment to a furniture store, I can use that money to fund my 401(k).

We have two choices when it comes to spending our money: we can use it to benefit ourselves and our families, or we can waste it and help someone else create wealth for their family.

Everything in life comes down to the choices that we make. We can choose to remain in debt, or we can choose to get out. We can choose to prepare for emergencies, or we can choose financial uncertainty. We can choose to prepare for retirement, or we can choose to struggle in our golden years.

Most advisors suggest, and I agree, that you should never invest in anything that you do not understand. Do not invest your money just because a person seems pleasant or is well dressed and charming; that does not make him right or honest. The first thing that people say when they have been taken advantage of is that "he (or she) seemed so sincere." Do your research and do not be afraid to ask questions, or consider paying a professional for guidance or recommendations.

Investing on a Budget:
<u>The Basics</u>

There are a number of places to put your money for retirement and basic savings: 401(k), Roth IRA, certificates of deposit, savings bonds, mutual funds, etc. Since investments can be very detailed, it is best to research and deal with a professional. I will only share with you the choices that I made when I started. I wanted to learn firsthand, so I choose simple investments that I could try out and follow for a year. After that, I could continue with the ones that worked best for my needs.

401(k)

I figured the best place to start investing was my home away from home: my place of employment. I invested in my 401(k), a defined retirement plan account. Through payroll deductions, I invested a percentage of my earnings before taxes were deducted, reducing my current taxable income which means I paid less federal taxes. My company also matched a percentage of my contributions.

There are two main types of IRAs (Individual Retirement Accounts):
Roth IRA

The main advantage of a Roth IRA, named for its chief legislative sponsor, the late Senator William Roth of Delaware, is its tax structure. If you meet certain requirements, earnings grow tax-free and distributions are *not* taxed upon withdrawal. There are, however, specific eligibilities and filing status requirements mandated by the Internal Revenue Service (IRS).

- You are allowed to open a Roth IRA if you have taxable earned income and qualify under the income limits. The Internal Revenue Service will only allow taxpayers who make less than a certain adjusted gross income to open a Roth IRA. Since there are no age restrictions, a Roth IRA may be a great savings vehicle for qualified teens working their first jobs.

- You will not receive a tax deduction for money that you use to open or to fund the account; the money must come from after-tax income.

- With a Roth IRA, if you still have earned income after age 70½, you may continue making contributions. You are also not required to take mandatory distributions at any age during your life.

- There are limits on the amount of money that you can contribute. If you are 50 years old or older and meet certain requirements, you can contribute more as a way to catch up on retirement savings. As with all investments, rules and regulations apply.

Traditional IRA

A Traditional IRA is a personal savings plan for your retirement. With a Traditional IRA, the government gives tax advantages for setting money aside for your retirement.

- You may be able to deduct your contributions, depending on your modified adjusted gross income and other requirements.

- Your earnings are tax-deferred until they are withdrawn. Because the Traditional IRA is a retirement vehicle, the Internal Revenue Service's (IRS) early withdrawal penalties may apply if you are under the age of 59½ when you withdraw money.

Certificates of Deposit (CDs)

A CD is a time deposit, meaning that CDs have a specific fixed term before the money can be withdrawn, often three months, six months, nine months, or up to five years.

CDs usually pay a fixed interest rate. You can hold CDs until they mature and then you can withdraw the money, including the accrued interest, or reinvest the money. One good thing about CDs is that you can stagger them to mature at different times. For example, you can purchase CDs for your major emergency fund, and have your CDs set up to mature every three months. You could purchase three-, six-, nine-, and twelve-month CDs. With a three-month cushion in your savings account, you could have CDs maturing every three months for a year or longer.

Savings Bonds

There are a number of different savings bonds to choose from. I chose to start with the series EE bonds.

Series EE Bonds are available for purchase in denominations of $50, $75, $100, $200, $500, $1,000, $5,000, or $10,000. You purchase Series EE savings bonds at half their face value. The bonds that I chose will take 17 years before they are worth their face value, a few years ahead of my retirement date. I like the idea that purchasing a bond each month will give me extra income during retirement. I also like the bonds that I chose, because in case of a financial emergency, I can turn them in (after a year) and get back my initial investment with interest. The interest is modest, but it is money that I would have wasted. Bonds also make great gifts for kids in place of toys for birthdays or holidays.

The minimum investment in a Series EE bond is $25 for a bond with a face value of $50. The maximum investment for a Series EE bond is $10,000 cash for a total face value of

$20,000. The library is full of books on bonds. Take advantage of it.

Mutual Funds

- A mutual fund is when thousands of small investors pool their money together to buy stocks, bonds, or other securities.

Every dollar is important when you are investing on a budget. Possible fees are commissions, loads, redemption fees, exchange fees, and account fees.

Fun and Interesting Information:
<u>The Rule of 72</u>

The Rule of 72 is a simple way to figure out the number of years it would take to double your money.

Simply take the interest rate that the financial company is offering and divide that number into "72."

Example:

Amount of time it will take a $5,000 investment to double:

- (Earning 4% interest) **72** divided by 4% = 18 years to double.

- (Earning 6% interest) **72** divided by 6% = 12 years to double.

- (Earning 8% interest) **72** divided by 8% = 9 years to double.

If you need to double your money in _x_ amount of years, to figure out the interest needed, you would simply divide the number of years _x_ into 72.

Example:

If you need to double your money in 6 years, take 72 and divide it by 6 = 12%.

You will need to earn about a 12% interest rate to double your $5,000 investment.

*This rule is assuming the interest is compounded annually.

*The rule of 72 is pretty accurate under a 20% interest rate. After that, the room for error becomes significant.

What Comes after a
<u>Trillion?</u>

(numbers to know)

Remember, the next time you hear these numbers being thrown out loosely, they could be talking about your tax dollars!

Our politicians and heads of companies make a million dollars sound like small change, when in fact it takes 10,000 <u>*one hundred-dollar bills*</u> to make a million dollars.

- It takes one thousand million-dollar stacks to make a billion dollars.

- It takes one thousand billion-dollar stacks to make a trillion dollars. *(The American debt is in the trillions!)*

If a trillion comes after a billion, what comes after a trillion?

- A <u>*quadrillion*</u> comes after a trillion in the good old U.S.A. *There are 15 zeros in a quadrillion.*

- It takes a thousand trillions to make a quadrillion.

The Magic of Compound Interest:
<u>Growing Your Money</u>

Albert Einstein said, "The most powerful force in the universe is compound interest." Given enough time and patience, even modest returns can generate wealth. The structure of compound interest is such that your money feeds on itself, first paying interest on your principal, then you will earn interest on the previous interest. For example, if you invest $1,000 (principal investment) at 5% compound interest:

- $1,000 earning 5% interest = $50. The $50 is added to the original principal: $1,000 + $50 = $1,050.

- The next time you earn interest you will earn interest on both the principal and the interest you previously earned. Your new principal amount is $1,050.

- You now have $1,050 earning 5% interest = $52.50. The $52.50 is added to your new principal amount: $1,050 + $52.50 = $1,102.50.

- Your new principal is $1,102.50 earning 5% interest = $55.13. The $55.13 is added to your new principal amount: $1,102.50 + $55.13 = $1,157.63.

The dark side of compound interest comes when you are paying interest instead of earning it.

Can You Afford to Double a
Penny for 30 Days?

Double a penny for 30 days — how hard can that be? Just pull out your wallet, get your hidden stash, and it is a done deal! Not so fast. If you double a penny a day for 30 days, you would have over five million dollars. How cool is that?

Day 1–10	Day 11–20	Day 21–30
.01	$10.24	$10,485.76
.02	$20.48	$20,971.52
.04	$40.96	$41,943.04
.08	$81.92	$83,886.08
.16	$163.84	$167,772.16
.32	$327.68	$335,544.32
.64	$655.36	$671,088.64
1.28	$1,310.72	$1,342,177.20
2.56	$2,621.44	$2,684,354.40
5.12	$5,242.88	**$5,368,708.80**

Chapter Four

Taking Charge:

Learning to Become the
<u>Boss of Your Money</u>

*"With each accomplishment,
you gain the confidence to take
another step."*

Lucille Baldwin

It Is Nothing Personal;
It Is Just Business: Yours!

"It's nothing personal. I am just trying to take care of my family, and I suggest that *you* try to take care of yours." This was a statement that a previous manager made to me during a performance evaluation. The problem started when I found out that my manager was not giving hourly employees raises based on job performance. A few weeks earlier, I received information that the company mistakenly faxed along with my paperwork. The memo reminded the management team that they would receive their yearly bonuses if they continued to keep company expenses down, which also included "employee salary dollars."

During my meeting with the store manager, one of my questions to him was, "How can you give me a *fair* evaluation and raise, if the company rewards you financially to keep salary dollars down?" If this were the case, then it was a conflict of interest. He suddenly became irate at my questions and tried to convince me that I was wrong, but I know what I read. After he stopped pounding his fist on the desk, and the color returned to his face, he began to calm down. I quietly left his office, leaving him to wipe the sweat from his brow. It was about an hour or so later that he came to me and made the above statement.

Many things have crossed my path that changed the way I view money. Nothing has affected my thinking more than that statement and my conversation with my manager. It taught me that people will do things that they know are unethical or unfair if it means keeping *their jobs* and taking care of *their families*. That moment taught me that we cannot always control the actions of others when it comes to our money, but we can control our own.

My manager's words remain with me today. When I sit at a desk to do business, those words remind me that the person sitting across from me is there to take care of their family. That means that I need to take my time and read the contracts, including the fine print. It means that if I need to wait and do additional research on the topic, then I do just that. It means that I do not commit to a deal or make a large purchase on impulse, no matter how much I love the item. It means that I take charge of my decisions and money in a way that benefits my situation and *my* family. It is nothing personal. It is just business: my business.

Your Money and Reality:
The True Spending Power of Your Money

One reason that we seem to spend beyond our means is that we have a false sense of the power of our income. We hear and see the *gross* amount of our pay and wrap our minds around that figure. Because our gross income is more appealing, it becomes hard to let go of that number, true or not. Choosing to block out the standard deductions and focusing only on the higher number, we mentally give our income too much spending power. Once you take a realistic look at your income, you get a clearer picture of how far your money can really go. Learning to become the boss of your money will mean "keeping it real," as the kids like to say. Keeping it real in adult terms means making decisions based on reality.

A few years ago, I was watching a popular talk show. The topic was financial management. Throughout the show, they allowed the studio and television audience to enter the financial lives of a few willing guests. What I remember most about the show was that one of the wives was a reckless spender.

The wife was an attractive stay-at-home mom with a beautiful little girl. She felt that because of her husband's high income, they could easily afford her spending habits. Just because they were in debt, she saw no reason not to enjoy lunch out with family and friends three to four days a week. Nor did she see any reason to stop her weekly shopping trips for new clothes and items for their beautiful new $500,000 home. Her husband earned $125,000 a year, and she was not ready to give up her spending habits without a fight.

The financial advisor organized the couple's finances and put together a budget for them. The wife had a hard time sticking with the budget. Although the family was struggling financially, she did not understand why she needed to curb her spending or give up her weekly trip to the salon with her daughter. Her mind was wrapped around the $125,000 that her husband was earning, and she did not want to let go of that sum.

Your Gross Income

- vs -

Your True Income

Gross Income: Your total income **before** taxes, retirement plans/401k, and other similar deductions. Most lenders ask for your gross income when you apply for a loan, giving you the false perception that you have more money to spend than you actually do.

Net Income: Your take-home pay **after** taxes and deductions such as life insurance, health insurance, dental, vision, and retirement plans have been taken out of your income.

Disposable Income: Money used for your necessary living expenses such as rent/mortgage, food, utilities, auto note, plus debt that you are legally responsible for repaying. Disposable income can also be used for saving.

Discretionary Income: Discretionary income is the money you have left over after you have paid your taxes, deductions, and living expenses. Discretionary income is the amount of money that you can either save or spend on non-essentials such as entertainment, cosmetics, collections, salon visits, golf clubs, etc.

If you want to take charge of your spending, knowing and accepting how much money is really available to spend will be necessary.

Before Signing a Contract,
<u>Slow Down and Relax</u>

When shopping for large ticket items, especially when there are contracts, payments, interest, and fees involved, slow down and relax. *Never* shop when you are in a hurry. When I sold cars, I was always amazed when people came in during their lunch break to conduct business, showing their lack of patience by rushing everyone to get things done in an hour. Making a decision in an hour or two that can affect your income for years is crazy. Do not rush yourself and do not allow anyone to pressure you into making a purchasing decision without giving you time to think it over.

After the salesperson has answered all of your questions, take time to read over the contract in private — *without* the salesperson, finance person, or anyone else involved standing over you. Remember, you will be responsible for making the payments, so you want the deal that is best for you and your family, not the deal that benefits the seller.

Never, Never
Sign Anything without Reading it First!

While telling us another joke to distract us, the salesperson hands us a pen and, without thinking, we have signed an important contract without reading it first.

Never, never, never (and I do mean never) sign anything without first *reading*, *understanding*, and *accepting* the terms of the contract. Asking questions is okay and is your right. If you need to ask a hundred questions, then ask a hundred questions; the money you save may be your own.

If they promise you anything, make sure that it is in writing with an authorized signature *before* you sign the contract. Salespeople can be very generous when they are trying to make the sale. They may not be as generous if later you realize that they "forgot" to add something to your contract that they verbally promised you.

Always, Always, Always
<u>Read the Fine Print</u>

Your contract includes a $5,000 final balloon payment. Your payments will increase by 25% in six months. We reserve the right to increase your interest for any reason at any time. There is no grace period and we will charge you a $39 late fee if we receive your payment after the due date.

What is the reason behind putting information in fine print? When companies want us to notice them, they have no problem using **large, bold** print. Using fine print may be a way for companies to steer us away from important information: information that may cause us to think twice about signing a contract or purchasing an item.

When we come across fine print, we sometimes disregard the information and move along to the next section, or worse, we may sign the contract without reading it. Guess what? You have done exactly what they wanted. The most important information can be found in the fine print. Like the fact that your interest could be 24% or that there is a $200.00 cancellation fee.

Do not sign first and read your contract later; by then it is too late. If you wait until you get home to read your contract and realize that you disagree with something, you will not have the opportunity to re-sign. Do not wait until you have a concern or problem with your purchase to read your contract. A signed contract carries a lot of weight legally. A judge will not care that you did not read or understand your contract.

During my daughter's last year of college, a friend of hers signed a contract after graduation to wear a well-known company's logo during his sports events. In his excitement he did not read the contract. He learned, thousands of dollars later, that he was financially responsible for paying his own travel expenses to and from the events. They also required him to pay for his uniforms, food, and several other expenses related to the sport. The deal did not benefit him, and he lost money by signing that contract.

Do not be fooled by salespeople. It is their job to be nice to you. It is their job to get you to relax and talk about yourself or your interests. It is their job to find a common bond so that you feel comfortable. It is, also, their job to make you feel like you are doing business with a friend. It is a lot easier to get a friend to sign a contract.

Once you become relaxed and comfortable with the salesperson, you are more likely to let down your guard because you trust that person. After all, you have so much in common! You have probably spent hours with this person and you trust him or her to have your best interest at heart. Most salespeople are nice and honest, but no matter how nice they are to you, no matter how much you have in common, do not sign without reading the contract, especially the fine print. The truth can normally be found in the fine print. You are there to do business, not to make a friend. Remember: It is nothing personal; it is just business!

Do Not Be Intimidated
by
<u>The "Hard-Sell" Style</u>

The hard sell is my least favorite style; I cannot tolerate the pressure. When I sold cars, my coworkers who enjoyed that technique considered themselves type-A personalities: aggressive, impatient, competitive, and rude — giving themselves an excuse for behaving badly. The worst experience is when you tell the salesperson no, and he gets his boss, and that boss gets her boss. The process can be very intimidating, but you must be firm: no means no. Do not be afraid to stand up and walk out of the office or ask for a different salesperson.

Time-Share:
A Bite of the Pie

It never fails, when I am on vacation I am offered certificates for free dinners or free tickets to local attractions. The best freebies are the two- or three-day getaways in a beautiful condo or villa, located in a romantic vacation resort. The gifts are not totally free; you are required to spend about 90 minutes watching a presentation or listening to a sales pitch on the benefits of owning your own "piece of heaven." This is normally when you will experience the hard sell. It seems that salespeople with the most confidence and intimidating style must all sell time-shares.

If they can afford to give away so many gifts, they must be making huge profits from time-share owners. Purchasing a time-share means that I would be helping to pay for all those gifts. I have friends and family members who have purchased time-shares and who share another common bond: at one time or another, they have *all* tried to sell their time-shares. (Correction: I have one close friend who paid cash for her time-share and she loves the experience.)

What is a time-share?

A time-share is not an asset, because you do not own the property. Try to paint the walls or change a light fixture, and you will find out who really owns the property when they send you a bill to reverse your work. When you purchase a time-share, you are paying for the *use* of a unit, normally a condominium or villa, in a recreational area. You can purchase as little as a week or months. The more time or points that you purchase, the more money you can expect to spend.

As a Time-Share Owner, You Are Also:

- Responsible for your share of monthly maintenance fees.

- Responsible for your share of property tax.

- Limited to the available areas where your company's time-shares are located.

- Limited by the available time slots.

- Paying for administrative fees.

- Paying for commissions to salespeople.

- Paying for gifts to entice new owners.

- Responsible for interest if you finance the purchase of your time-share.

If you like the idea of purchasing a time-share, it may be a good idea to research re-sales or foreclosures. Be careful that you do not purchase a time-share on impulse while you are on vacation. Buying a time-share can be an expensive souvenir. Be strong! Do not be intimidated by the hard sell.

A Few Questions to Ask Yourself
Before You
<u>Consider a Time-Share</u>

(A time-share is a luxury, not a necessity.)

Have you paid off your primary mortgage?

Have you fully funded or started a retirement account?

Have you funded your emergency account (6 to 12 months of living expenses)?

Do you already have other consumer debt (credit cards, auto loans, student loans, etc.)?

Can you afford to pay cash for the time-share?

What is the total cost of purchasing a time-share (fees, interest)?

Do the benefits of owning a time-share outweigh the monthly mortgage payment, monthly maintenance fee, and property tax?

Why are so many time-share owners selling?

Have you researched time-share resales by owners?

Have you researched purchasing a time-share that has gone through a foreclosure?

Purchasing Your Dream Home
(Are You Ready?)

Can you really buy a home for the same amount as you pay in rent every month? When people are trying to earn your business, they may not always be totally honest. They may not come out and tell you a lie; they may just omit vital information. It is nothing personal; it is a survival instinct. They have bills to pay and their own families to feed.

I have been a home renter all my life, but a couple of years ago, I considered becoming a first-time homebuyer. My realtor told me that I could purchase a home paying the same amount of money that I paid in rent. At that point in my life, I was learning not to take everything at face value and to check out the facts. My first step was to take a homebuyers' class.

I believe in the American Dream and the pride of ownership. I also believe that you should prepare financially for that dream. The main lesson that I learned on my journey was that I was not yet prepared to become a homeowner. The first steps that I needed to take toward purchasing a home were to get out of debt, improve my credit score to get the best rate, and to come up with ways to earn additional income.

The second lesson that I learned was that buying a home was *not* the same as renting a home, and it could not be done for the same amount of money. It is a lesson that I am happy I learned before, rather than after, signing a contract. The next time I come to the table to purchase a home, I plan to bring a little more knowledge about the process, excellent credit, at least a 20% down payment, and enough sense to know my buying power.

What They Forgot to Tell Me about Ownership:
<u>Renting - vs - Owning</u>

Buying a Home

Down payment (The less money you put down, the larger your mortgage payment.)

Mortgage Payment

Property Tax

Homeowner's Insurance

Private Mortgage Insurance (PMI is mandatory if you put down less than 20% or have less than 20% equity in your home.)

Utilities may include electricity, water, sewer, trash pickup, cable, etc. The larger the home, the higher the utilities. (The city put up a lamppost in front of a coworker's home and mailed her the bill.)

Maintenance and Repair Costs (If the roof leaks, the air conditioner needs replacing, or the refrigerator stops working, as the "homeowner" you are now responsible for the repairs.)

Home Owner's Association Fees (HOA fees are separate fees for amenities. Amenities may include shared common areas such as a pool, recreation room, a park, exercise room, etc. Some communities charge an HOA fee and only maintain the grounds. When they were called apartments, that service was included. This is a fee normally found with condos, townhomes, or gated communities; the monthly fees can be very hefty, costing hundreds of dollars a month.)

Interest (An older woman that I know has a modest home; she took out a *$100,000* loan. The monthly payment on her loan is $764 a month, for thirty years. $764 x 12 months = $9,168 a year in payments. $9,168 x 30 years = *$275,040*. She will almost pay for her house three times.)

Another couple purchased a home for $213,000. They have a monthly payment of $1,390 for thirty years. $1,390 x 12 months = $16,680 a year. $16,680 x 30 years = $500,400.

Renting a Home

Deposit (normally the amount of the first and last month's rent)

Monthly Rent

Utilities (sometimes water, cable, or heat may be included)

If the hot water heater leaks, you call the owner/site manager.

If the plumbing backs up, you call the owner or site manager.

If you have a maintenance concern, it is the owner's problem.

The American Dream of home ownership is a beautiful thing and well within reach for all of us. It is not a dream to enter into lightly — without planning and preparation. I always hear people say that they are homeowners, but in reality the bank or mortgage company owns the home until they make the final payment and receive the deed. When purchasing your Dream Home, be realistic and stay within your means. Someone working on commission may try to convince you to buy more than your wallet can handle. You know your responsibilities and what you can afford.

Whole Life - vs - Term Life:
Life Insurance

The main purpose of life insurance is to protect the people that depend on your income to support their needs. This may include the roof over their heads, the food in their mouths, child care expenses, education, and even the shoes on their feet. What would happen to your family if they lost not only you, but also the income that you provide?

We may not realize how important life insurance is until we are in an accident or become ill; suddenly, we are reminded that a long and healthy life is not promised. Taking the time to research life insurance, and figuring out which type is best for you and your family, is well worth the time and energy that you invest.

Do not just take the word of an insurance agent because he stands to make money to sell you a life insurance policy. You control the decision by reading, and reading some more, about the different types of life insurance policies that are available to you.

Ask yourself if you need life insurance. Who is depending on your income for support? How much insurance coverage do you need? How much insurance can you afford? Do you need life insurance coverage for the parent that stays home to raise the children? Will you need to hire someone to do the work that the stay-at-home parent is providing for the family? You may not realize the value that a person brings to the home, until he or she is no longer in your life. There are different types of life insurance policies available to you. Take the time to find the policy that is best for your family.

Temporary Life Insurance

Temporary life insurance, best known as term life insurance, is just what the name implies: temporary, or for a limited time. You may have children and want life insurance to keep them protected until they become adults or are out of college.

Term insurance, also referred to as pure insurance, can be purchased in increments from 1 to 30 years (a block of time that best serves your family). If you have a five-year-old, you may want term insurance for 20 years until he or she completes college.

Premiums (payments) can be made monthly, quarterly, semi-annually, or annually.

Term insurance will pay your beneficiary the face value of the policy when you die. A $200,000 policy pays $200,000. You do not have to receive the lump sum; you can research and talk with an agent about receiving a monthly payment from interest.

Term life insurance costs less than whole life insurance.

The three types of term life insurances are <u>level term, annual renewable term</u>, and <u>decreasing term</u>.

<u>**Level term**</u> payments will remain the same for the life of the policy. The face value of the policy remains the same.

<u>**Annual renewable,**</u> as the name implies, can be renewed each year. Term premiums increase as you get older.

<u>**Decreasing term**</u> means the face value of the policy decreases, while the premiums remain the same.

Whole Life Insurance

Whole life insurance covers you for the duration of your life, as long as you keep up with your premiums and your policy has not been cancelled. Whole life insurance is more expensive because it includes an investment vehicle that builds a cash value. You can borrow against the cash value, *but* that is equivalent to borrowing your own money and paying someone else interest. It also takes years to build up a decent cash value.

The three types of Permanent/Whole Life Insurances are traditional whole life, universal life, and variable life.

Traditional Life Insurance

Combines an insurance policy with an investment vehicle.

High commission and fees are paid to the agent.

Premiums may be several times higher than term insurance.

Premiums will not increase.

Universal Life Insurance

Offers payment flexibility.

Payments can be skipped.

Earns interest.

Premiums are lower than whole life.

Guaranteed to earn policy minimum in interest.

It is possible to earn a higher rate than the guaranteed rate.

Premiums could increase.

Variable Life Insurance

Higher risk.

Greatest potential for cash value increase, but no guarantees.

Most advisors prefer term insurance to whole life insurance. Do your research to find the insurance that works best for you and your family. I prefer term insurance because I get more coverage for my money. Because I did not understand the difference, for years I paid extra money for whole life insurance.

Child Rider Policy

A child rider insurance policy allows you to add a child to your policy for a small additional fee to cover the cost of a funeral and possible time missed from work.

Return of Premium Policy

The return of premium policy is one in which you purchase a policy for a set amount of time such as 30 years. You pay your premiums every year, and if you die, your beneficiaries will receive the face value of your policy. If you do not die within the 30 years, you will receive the full amount that you paid in premiums tax-free. How can you lose with this type of policy? The insurance company is in business to make money, not to give it away: the price for this type of policy may be two to four times the price of a standard policy.

Mortgage Life Insurance

Normally purchased by new homeowners.

A fancy name for life insurance.

Very expensive. Much more than regular life insurance.

Premiums will not increase.

Death payment may go to the mortgage company instead of family.

Disability Insurance

What is disability insurance?

Disability insurance is insurance on your ability to earn an income. It will pay you a portion of your income if you become unable to work due to an illness or accident. It will not, however, replace 100% of your lost wages; disability insurance will cover about 45% to 70% of your gross income, tax-free.

The purpose of disability insurance is to give you peace of mind in the event that you are injured or become ill. You do not want to worry about your rent or mortgage falling behind, or debt piling up while you are out of work. The purchasing of disability insurance is important and should be checked out to find the company and coverage that meets your needs.

There Are Two Types of Disability Insurances:

Short-Term Disability

Zero to 14 days waiting period before receiving payout.

Maximum payout of about one to two years.

Long-Term Disability

Possible waiting period of several weeks or several months.

Maximum benefit period could range from a few years to the remainder of your life.

Do You Need Disability Insurance?

Are you the head of your household? If you suffer an illness or accident that prevents you from working for a few months or years, would it put a strain on your ability to pay your bills? How much money would you need to handle your monthly expenses?

Life insurance is purchased to protect your loved ones from financial devastation in the event of your death. In reality, you stand a better chance of losing time from work due to an illness or accident. The loss of income can be draining, not only on your ability to run your household, but also to your family's sense of security.

Insurance Questions to Keep in Mind:

Do you have group disability insurance with your employer?

Do you have a policy that the insurance company cannot cancel except for nonpayment of premiums?

Do you have a guaranteed right to renew your policy without an increase in your premiums or a reduction in your benefits?

Is there a benefit cap?

What is the length of the coverage? If you become ill for years, how long will you be covered?

How does the policy handle recurring periods of disability that occur within a 12-month period from the same or related causes?

How does the policy define disability?

Does the policy offer a rehabilitation benefit?

Will you be able to, or forced to, work part-time with a partial disability option?

Is the policy portable? Will you be able to take the policy with you if you change jobs?

Until Death, Divorce, or Abandonment
Do Us Part
(Fairy Tales and a "Cinderella" Mentality)

Once upon a time, I believed in fairy tales. I was raised with wonderful stories of *Cinderella, Snow White*, and other classic tales. Through books and movies, I learned to believe that love conquers all, and to always be on the lookout for my one true love. I had faith that if you believed in love and soul mates, that life would fall into place. My prince charming would ride up on his white horse, swoop me up, and together we would ride off into the sunset, living happily ever after.

I thought that I met my prince charming; he was tall, dark, and handsome, just like in the books and he only lived five blocks away. High school sweethearts, we would walk hand in hand under the stars, planning our future. Years later, we were married with two beautiful little girls living out my dream. According to the script, life would be perfect: our children would behave like the children from *The Brady Bunch* and *Leave It to Beaver* television shows. For awhile I thought life was perfect, but I was a naive young woman playing house and "cooking" hamburger meals and calling it dinner.

Disciplining our children would never be a problem for us. After all, the children on television only needed a little time to reflect on their bad behavior. We would send our children to their rooms to think about what they had done. They would return a short time later, filled with sorrow and apologize for their misdeeds. We would forgive them and share a family hug. The next chapter in my fantasy was of my husband and myself sitting in our rocking chairs on the front porch, sipping lemonade. We would live happily ever after watching our grandchildren playing in the yard. The fantasy in my head always ended with that scene.

The problem with my childhood fantasy of marriage was that reality stepped in and surrounded me. My children did not come close to behaving like the kids from the television shows. My prince charming abandoned his white horse, and my rose-colored glasses were shattered as real life set in. Seven years later, my not-so-storybook marriage ended in divorce, and I went from Mrs. to Ms. My fantasy never included a divorce or raising my children alone.

This was not the way the stories ended in the fairy tales that were read to me as a child or shown on the big screen. The books that I read and the movies that I watched promised me a happy ending. The reality is that scripts can change, and "happily ever after" is not written in stone. I was alone with two young children, a part-time job, no savings, and no child-support income. I had become a statistic. Looking back at that woman-child, I realized that at 21 she was not prepared for marriage.

The Burden of a Breakup:
<u>For the Sake of the Children, Prepare!</u>

The negative statistics of the financial effects divorce has on our children are overwhelming. We watch movie stars and athletes go through divorces and form a belief that women have it easy after a breakup, with their ex-husbands footing the bills. The reality is that after a divorce a number of women, with their children in tow, can expect their income level to drop by as much as 50%, plunging them into poverty. On the flip side, the divorcing husband's income can increase by 25%, with his quality of life improving.

Sadly, a divorcing woman may or may not receive child support. It is an unfortunate truth that only about 50% of all court-ordered child support is received, and only 25% of that is paid in full. I qualified for child support over twenty years ago, and I am still waiting for my first check.

Because of a drop in income, women and children are sometimes forced to move out of their homes. Adding to the devastation of a family breakup, children may also be required to change schools, leaving behind friends and teachers.

I learned the hard way that even if you think you have found your prince charming, it is important for women to educate and empower themselves with financial information. It is not only divorce or abandonment that can cause financial devastation, but the fact that women tend to outlive their husbands and are not preparing for the future.

Do not wait until you are faced with a devastating situation to learn how to balance a checkbook, pay bills, or what it takes to run a household. Raised with fairy tales and love stories, it is easy to get swept up in the mystery of romance, expecting the power of love to protect us from all situations.

As intelligent women, we cannot continue to allow love to blind us from the realities of life or convince us to bury common sense. We give our fantasies of love too much power. Depending on love, we unknowingly set ourselves up for failure by relying too heavily on our husbands or partners for financial support.

It is common for women to stay at home and raise the children and assume that our husbands or partners will take care of us forever. Living this lifestyle, we spend fewer years in the workforce and take jobs where we earn less money than men, reducing our retirement income. We do not worry that with the gaps in our work history and working at lower paying jobs we are neglecting our retirement accounts. Again, we are assuming that our husbands will provide for our future.

What I have learned and tried to pass down to my own daughters is that it is okay to fall in love and still have a separate checking account. It is okay to be in love and still build and maintain excellent credit. You can be in love, have an emergency account, purchase assets, and be in control of your life and finances. You can believe in "happily ever after" while maintaining your independence and handling your financial affairs.

In real life, the road to "happily ever after" is not guaranteed. As women and mothers it is important that we prepare in the event our lives take a detour. We all think that the death of a spouse, a breakup, or abandonment will not happen to us, but we cannot all be right.

Another important lesson that I learned and passed down to my daughters is that it is okay to enjoy being single, travel the world, and never have 2.5 children. Becoming a wife and mother are not our only options. There is nothing like being self-reliant. Love hard, plan well, and by all means handle your business!

So, You Wanna Buy a Car?

Good Credit - Bad Credit -
No Credit - No Problem!

No Money Down* Payments as Low as $99 a Month*

$3,000 Minimum for Your Trade *

Push it - Pull it - Drag it - Tow it - Just Get it Here

A gimmick is a trick or device intended to attract attention rather than fulfill a useful purpose. "Bring in your winning letter, number, or flyer and you could be a winner!" Beware of brightly colored ads/gimmicks offering deals that seem too good to be true. How is it possible to have bad credit and qualify for a $20,000 vehicle with no money down and low monthly payments? The odds are that it is not possible. Avoid tent sales, inventory reduction sales, bank sales, and similar advertisements. The circus-like atmosphere, the smell of fresh popcorn, and the free drinks are to entice impulse buying versus smart buying.

The main purpose of auto ads offering unrealistic deals is to attract as many potential buyers into the dealership as possible. Selling cars is a numbers' game. The more people that flock into the dealership, the greater the odds of selling a vehicle. Most of us will overlook the asterisk (*) or other pointer symbols directing us to the fine print and the _truth_ behind the gimmick. We jump into our cars or catch a ride with a friend to the dealership to take advantage of a great opportunity to purchase a vehicle.

The problem starts when we get to the dealership with our bad credit and empty wallets. That is when the salesperson points to the bottom of the ad and asks you if you read the fine print. He tells you that those offers only apply to people *with approved credit,* which is the meaning of the W.A.C.* in the ad that you overlooked. He wants to know if *you* have excellent credit. The salesperson informs you that although your credit is not so great, with $2,000 or $3,000 down, he can still get you into a nice vehicle.

You tell him that you are unable to come up with the $2,000 or $3,000 needed to buy a vehicle. He thinks for a moment, then he says: "Let me ask you a question: is there anyone in your family who loves you and cares enough about you to co-sign a loan for you?" "Maybe my grandmother," you tell him. He points to a chair in his office and tells you to have a seat and he will give your grandmother a call.

If it seems too good to be true, break out your reading glasses or a magnifying glass and look for the fine print. Purchasing a vehicle is the largest purchase for most people, second only to purchasing a home. Take your time. If you have bad credit and can wait until you bring up your score before purchasing a car, you can save a great deal of money on interest.

Before You Visit the Dealership
Do Your Research!

How do you plan on paying for your car? Can you afford to pay cash? Do you have money for a down payment? Will you need to borrow money to purchase a vehicle? Before you commit yourself and your future earnings to five, six, or even seven years' worth of monthly payments, consider the reality of such a commitment. The reality: If you need that much time to pay for a car, you are buying a vehicle that is beyond your means.

Stretching your payments out for a longer period may seem like a good idea. You get your dream vehicle with what feels like affordable payments. Life is good... until your family grows and you need to trade in your car for a larger model. By making small payments, you increase your chances of becoming "upside down" on your loan, which means you owe more than your car is worth. With negative equity, it may be difficult or more expensive to qualify for a new loan.

You are not what you drive! Do not throw your money away purchasing an expensive car that you cannot afford. A car will depreciate by about 25% the moment you drive off the lot. We would not walk past a trash can and toss in money or our paycheck. Yet we think nothing of investing years paying for a vehicle because we love the color, or it makes us feel special. You do not need to become tied down to a car that you cannot afford to prove that you are special. When purchasing a car, buy the car that you need, until you can afford the car that you want.

- Take advantage of all the information at your disposal. Make time to research car-buying tips. You had better believe that the salespeople and finance officers are taking classes on how to make the best deal for the dealership.

- Shop around and compare models and prices.

- Salespeople are trained to distract you from the price of the car and try to get you to focus on the payment. Do not be a payment buyer.

- Come to an agreement on a fair price for the car. Let the salesperson know that you do not want to discuss payments until you agree on a purchase price. I met one couple who told the salesperson how much they wanted to pay monthly for a vehicle. Because the couple did not know the price of the car, the finance manager was able to increase the price of the car to match the payment they wanted.

- Check the history of the vehicle you are considering. If you do not ask, the dealer is not required to tell you about the history of the car or if it has been in an accident.

- Hire a mechanic that you trust to put the car on a lift and check it out. Also, talk with the mechanic about parts and labor. How expensive is the model you are considering to repair and maintain? My youngest daughter paid a mechanic $25 to check out a pre-owned vehicle before she made her final decision. It turned out that the car had a serious oil leak and needed about $2,500 worth of repairs; needless to say she did not buy the car.

- Secure financing ahead of time if possible. You may be able to get a better rate with the bank or at least an idea of your interest charge.

- Check auto insurance rates on the vehicle you are

considering before making your decision. I once sold a car to a young man, whose car note was $275, and his insurance payment was $520 a month; he was 22 and the car he purchased was considered a sports car.

- Do not forget to check on property tax for your state (not the same as sales tax on the car). You do not want to be surprised with a bill for property tax after you purchase your car.

- Do not sign a bill of sale with blanks or contracts that read "subject to bank approval." Dealers will sometimes allow you to take the vehicle home before the bank approves the loan. The salesperson will then call you to return the car because the *original loan fell through,* or to sign new paperwork, costing you more money.

- Before signing the "AS IS CONTRACT," be sure to check out the car completely and have a mechanic check it out. Test drive it for at least 30 minutes and take it on a road that will allow you to drive over 30 mph. I have been in cars that were fine at 30 mph but started shaking like crazy at 55 mph. Once you sign the "as is" contract, you cannot come back if you notice that the tires are not safe.

- Get *all* verbal promises in writing with an authorized signature.

- Kelley Blue Book or N.A.D.A. is available to get an idea of the value of your trade.

- Retrieve your keys after they complete the test drive and assessment on your trade. Some salespeople will "misplace" your keys to prevent you from leaving, trying to give themselves a little more time to convince you to buy a car.

- If you trade in a car that has a balance, make sure the dealer puts in writing that they will pay off your trade within 10 days. I know a couple that traded in their car and the dealership took three months to pay off the balance. Because the car was still in the couple's names, they continued receiving delinquent payment calls and letters from the loan company.

- You are responsible for the remaining balance on your trade. If you owe $8,000 on your trade and the dealer gives you $5,000, the remaining $3,000 will be *added* to your new loan.

- Know how much your trade is worth ahead of time.

- If you are just looking, do not give your telephone number to the salesperson unless you want to receive calls for the next year.

Do Not Fall for Lines Like:

- "I am trying to help you to rebuild your credit. The only way to rebuild your bad credit is to purchase a car and have it financed." This statement is not true; you do not need to purchase a car to rebuild your credit.

- "They just sold the car in the advertisement, but we have another great car that is just a little more expensive." The "Bait and Switch" move.

- "The payments are high, but if you pay on time for six months you can refinance your car with us and get lower payments." Do not believe it unless they are willing to put it in writing, which they are not. So, do not pay more than you can afford.

- "Today is the last day to take advantage of that price."

- "We have another buyer interested in purchasing this car." If they do have another buyer, there are other cars.

- "We have a buyer looking for a trade like yours."

- "We need to keep your trade overnight to assess the value." These are just tactics to put you in their vehicle overnight hoping that you "fall in love" with the car, increasing the chances that you will purchase it.

- "If I can get you a payment that you can afford, can I earn your business right now?" The job of the salesperson is to get you to buy a car the same day you walk into the dealership. They do not want you to leave and go to another dealership or take time to think it over.

- "It is less expensive to purchase a warranty from the dealership." In reality, the markups on warranties are almost *double* at dealerships. I never purchase the warranties anymore because they never covered my repairs. I put the money into an emergency account for when I need car repair.

- "Everything, and I do mean *everything*, is covered under this warranty." Only believe what is in writing.

- "You are required to purchase life insurance or a warranty to get the loan." Not true.

- To file a complaint, contact the Better Business Bureau at www.BBB.com and file a complaint through your Attorney General's website.

The Payment Increase Trick

You have a payment in mind that you do not want to go above when looking for your vehicle. The salesperson wants to get you to mentally increase your limit at least twice. You tell the salesperson that your payment should not exceed $300 a month. The salesperson will ask, "How much more can you afford if you *had* to?" Your response may be to say "$350." The salesperson may ask, "If we find your dream car and you really had to push it, how much more can you pay?" Your next response may be to say, "$450, and that's final."

In less than two minutes, you have increased the maximum amount that you wanted to pay. If you are not careful, you can walk away paying hundreds of dollars more per month than you intended. The salespeople are trained and coached to encourage you to purchase a car and spend beyond your set limit. Stick to your budget.

The Last Stop:
<u>The Finance Office</u>

The last step in the car-buying process is to sign all the paperwork and make the deal binding. This is where you will need to pull out your confidence, reading glasses, and calculator. Before you enter the finance office, *you* should have a good idea of the <u>total</u> cost of your vehicle. The total should include the price of your vehicle, state tax, tags, fees, and the cost for financing (interest rate).

Do not be intimidated by the finance manager. He or she will not be making your payments for you. Sometimes it is comforting to have a good friend or family member with you for support. Do not, under any circumstances, sign the contract without reading it from top to bottom. Flip it over to make sure there is nothing on the back of the contract. Search the contract for "add-ons." Add-ons include insurance, warranties, fabric protection, undercoating, paint protection, VIN etching, etc.

I went with my daughter to the dealership when she purchased her SUV. We walked into the finance office, satisfied with the vehicle, the price, the interest rate, and the monthly payment. She had already informed the salesperson that she did not want her payments to exceed $300. Once inside the finance office, I noticed that the final total on the contract was more than $4,000 higher than the total that I figured. The finance manager "added on" insurance and a warranty to the contract, without my daughter's permission, for an additional $4,200. This is called "payment packing." The customer qualifies for a $250 payment, tells the salesperson they do not want to pay over $300, the finance manager may add on enough items to take the payment up to $300, which is exactly what he did.

The finance manager kept the contract slightly above my daughter's target payment of $300. When it comes time to sign your contract, look beyond the payment. The manager said to me that "most people just sign the contract without reading it." He apologized for the misunderstanding and removed the insurance and warranty from the contract (she decided to keep one item). Reading the contract reduced her monthly payments to $250 and saved her $3,500.

- Beware of menu add-ons. This happens when the finance manager groups add-ons into packages and gives them fancy names. These add-on packages can increase your monthly payment by $30, $60, or $90. An additional $90 on a 60-month loan is more than $5,000. The finance manager is counting on you choosing one and not thinking about the offer. It is okay to say no!

- Have an idea of what to expect before you go into the finance office. *Price of vehicle* + *tax*, *tags* + *warranty* + *insurance* + *fees* + *cost of financing* = *Total*. Compare your total to the total on the contract.

- Have a copy of your credit history and know your credit score. Knowing your credit score will help you find the "credit tier" that you should fall under and give you an idea of the interest rate you should qualify for. Make sure your credit report is correct before the bank sees it. The salesperson and the finance manager should not know more about your credit history than you do.

- Payment calculators are available online. Once you know your credit score and credit tier, a payment calculator can give you an idea of the monthly payment you can expect.

- The better your credit and the closer the car price is to the invoice for a new car, or book value on a used car, the lower your financing rate. Meaning: The closer the car is to a fair price, the better it is for you and your wallet.

- Some dealers will allow you to leave the lot with a vehicle knowing that it has not been financed and the deal is "subject to final approval."

- In some states you are allowed to ask to see the seller's invoice to know how much profit the dealer stands to make.

- If you are interested in purchasing a warranty, know what it covers and what it does not cover before you buy the warranty. They should have a warranty book that you can read before you go into the finance office. If they do not want to give you the information ahead of time, take your time and read through the book in the finance office.

- Be careful when using a co-signer. Some finance managers will put the car in the co-signer's name instead of yours, without telling you.

- If you are a consumer under the age of 25, you may be denied a loaner car while your car is being serviced because of your age. Check the terms ahead of time.

There are thousands of dollars on the table; the finance office is not the time to be shy or become intimidated. Do your research and be an informed buyer.

A New Vehicle: Trading Up
"Out with the Old and In with the New"

I wanted to buy a new car and trade in my old vehicle, but I was told that I owed too much money on my old vehicle. What does that mean? Being upside down on your auto loan means that you owe the lender more money than your vehicle is worth. I make my payments on time. How could this happen?

Let's go back to the beginning. The advertisement that caught your eye read, "At least $3,000 for your trade! Push it, pull it, or tow it." It was not necessary for you to push, pull, or even tow your car to the dealership, but it was starting to give you trouble. The $3,000 that they promised for your trade would make an attractive down payment toward a newer vehicle. The trouble starts because you still owe the bank $6,000 on your old vehicle. You found a car that you love with a sticker price of $20,000.

Sticker Price .... $20,000.

Balance on Trade .... 6,000. (You are responsible for the remaining balance on trade.)

Dealer Fee .... 500. (Dealerships may charge fees.)

Property Tax .... 300. (The tax may be higher in other states.)

Auto Tags.................. 50. (Charges vary by state.)

Warranty .... 4,500. (Different prices and warranty choices)

Gap Insurance .... + 800.

Sub-Total ....$32,150.

Trade Allowance........$- 3,000.

Loan Amount.............$29,150.
                    This does not include interest!

We always hear how cars lose value as soon as you pull off the lot. So if your $20,000 car loses 25% when you pull off the lot, it is now worth $15,000.

*You owe $29,150 plus interest on your new car.

*Your new car is now worth $15,000!

That is how we become upside down in our car loan.

A Lack of Financial Knowledge
Attracts Predators!

<u>(Payday Loans - Title Loans - Check Cashing - Rent to Own)</u>

A lack of financial knowledge creates victims. It also attracts predators who target people with limited financial knowledge. To find the best hunting ground, these predators spend a great deal of money researching the best areas to find their prey. Their research suggests that they target the working poor, retired poor, minorities, college students, and members of the armed forces.

Like those predators, we need to handle business. Our strongest protection against financial predators is to increase our financial knowledge. There are more predators crawling out of the cracks every day, and the use of knowledge is a powerful defense against them. People can only take advantage of us if we allow it; our actions teach people how to treat us. Preparing for emergencies is the best way to avoid these types of companies.

What is a payday loan?

A payday loan is a short-term loan for a small dollar amount where the person who borrows the money promises to repay the loan out of their next paycheck. They can pay cash and pick up their check, or allow the funds to be withdrawn from their account.

How does a payday loan work?

The borrower (whom we will call Ann) writes a post-dated check to the loan company for the amount she needs, plus any fees charged by the company. Ann, a single mother of two, needs to replace worn tires and the brakes on her car at a cost of $400.

If, for example, the initial loan is for $400 for two weeks, and the fee is $60 *($15 per $100)*, Ann will make the check out for $460.

Most borrowers like Ann are unable to repay the loan when they receive their paycheck because of other obligations, and must take out another loan to repay the first loan. The second loan includes another $60 fee. The fee for the $400 loan will now cost $120.

The average borrower like Ann may "refinance" up to nine times per year. This type of borrowing is called *the loan rollover* or *debt trap*. If Ann needed the average amount of time to repay her loan, it will cost her $540 in fees.

<u>$400 initial loan amount + $540 fees = $940</u>

What is a car title loan?

A title loan or car title loan is one in which the borrower uses their car as collateral. If you fail to repay the loan, you will lose your car.

How does a car title loan work?

To keep things simple, we will have Ann join us again. A car title loan is similar to a payday loan in that it is for a short term and it has a high interest rate. Ann uses her car as collateral for the loan and gives the company a second set of keys and her title. If Ann is unable to repay and defaults on the loan, then the lender will take possession of her car.

Some companies may install a tracking device or take possession of the car during the life of the loan. If a borrower fails to keep up with her payments, it is also possible for some lenders to remotely disable a car's ignition. I met one lady who took out a car title loan for $1,000. After making three payments of $120 for a total of $360, three months later her new balance was $980. Only $20 out of $360 went toward paying down her balance! No need to tell you that she was not happy.

What are check cashers?

Check-cashing companies are in the same family as payday loan and title loan companies. They target low income customers who are normally not affiliated with a financial institution and have little or no cash reserve. Their customers (like Ann) are also charged high fees to use their services.

These companies sometimes offer other expensive services such as money transfers, lottery tickets, money orders, prepaid cell phones, prepaid debit cards, etc. If you qualify for membership with a regular bank or credit union, you may want to check into becoming a member. Handling your banking needs with a traditional bank or credit union can be less expensive.

Is renting to own a good idea?

Renting to own is another way to throw away your future wealth. When I was first married, my husband purchased a 13-inch color television set from a rent-to-own store. I could not convince him to save the money and purchase the same exact television from the retail store that was next door!

He followed his heart, obviously not his head, and purchased the television through the rent-to-own company. That television ended up costing him $1,300, four times the price of the television at the retail store. Can you believe it — $1,300 for a 13-inch television? To his credit, he never purchased another item that way.

He was enticed by the idea of "no money down, no credit check," and the fact that he could bring the television home the same day. To my ex-husband, his payments seemed small because he made weekly payments versus one larger monthly payment.

In his excitement to bring the television home, he overlooked the most important factor in the deal: the total cost of the television. Rent-to-own companies are similar to the other companies on the list because they prey on people with bad credit and low income. They charge high interest rates and may penalize you for paying off your account early. Respect your money and spend it wisely. Once again, research the deal before you commit and sign a contract. Stop being a target! Stop making the people that are taking advantage of you wealthy!

Chapter Five

Running Your Household:

<u>What You Don't Know</u> <u>Can Cost You!</u>

"By learning you will teach;
by teaching you will learn."

Latin Proverb

What You Don't Know
Can Cost You

I have often heard people say, "What you don't know cannot hurt you," or that ignorance is bliss. All I can say: *Do not believe it!* I will even go a step further by saying that what you do not know can cost you — in time and money. A lack of financial information and not understanding basic financial terms can cost you thousands of dollars in fees, interest, and poor choices. Somewhere along the way, we must realize that what we do not know *can* hurt us, and that ignorance is not always bliss. This realization gave me the power and confidence to choose a different path. The cost of financial ignorance may be high, but at least the remedy is free: time and a willingness to learn.

Making the best decisions for your household without basic information can be difficult. How do you choose between a fixed-rate loan and an adjustable-rate loan if you do not know the difference? How do you avoid wasting money on liabilities if you do not realize that you are doing it? How can you take advantage of compound interest if you have never heard of it? When I think back to the way that I ran my household, I am reminded of the houses that I built as a child, using wooden blocks. Without a solid foundation, it did not take much for those blocks to come crashing down around me. When I became an adult, I was still trying to build my home without a strong foundation. It turned out that financial knowledge was the material that I was missing to build the foundation.

On my journey, I came across the most interesting term: the "rational ignorance effect." Someone came up with this cool name for the negative way that we sometimes make decisions. The rational ignorance effect is when we purposely, or unconsciously, choose *not* to educate ourselves about an issue. If we do not believe that the time and effort needed to educate ourselves is worth the information gained, we may choose to forgo the information. Whether we want to admit it or not, it is a lot easier to remain clueless about an issue than it is to do the work.

We can, at times, be a lazy bunch. Instead of choosing to educate ourselves, we simply choose to put our trust in another person. Why else would we sign contracts that we do not understand or skip over terms that are not familiar to us? We put our trust in people who stand to make a profit from the contracts that we sign. Our only requirement of them is that they highlight or point to the line where they want us to sign. We blindly sign contracts, then sit back and smile, confident that we have done our part to protect our best interests. Then we label ourselves as victims when we later discover that they have taken advantage of us.

Sometimes, when we listen to people with degrees in economics or watch stockbrokers on television, we become intimidated by money; the process seems so overwhelming. A degree in economics or a diploma from an Ivy League university is not necessary to run our lives without creating debt. For most of us, the same basic money management terms and similar life experiences will cross our paths. How we choose to handle those situations is what will separate us on the road and determine our future.

We have the power to create and maintain the life that we want. For those of *us* who are willing to put forth the time and effort, we will reap the rewards of that work. For those of *you* who choose to remain on the same path, you will continue to struggle and blame others for your struggle. As always, the choice is yours!

Basic Financial Terms for
Everyday Living
(When You Are Not Born with a Silver Spoon)

Know these basic financial terms for everyday living to help make better spending and saving choices. The following terms have crossed my path over the years.

What is personal finance?

Personal finance is <u>the way that you manage your household money</u>: the way that you pay your bills, save, invest, etc.

What is a budget?

A budget is a detailed <u>schedule of your spending</u>. A budget is a tool to help you take charge of the money that you have coming in and out of your household.

What is an asset?

An asset is <u>something of *value* that you own and can exchange for cash</u>, in a financial emergency, during retirement, or anytime you need extra money. The more assets you purchase, the stronger your foundation, so waste less money and purchase more assets.

Examples of assets:

- stocks

- bonds

- certificates of deposits

- mutual funds

- retirement accounts

- annuities

- property that generates income such as real estate, rental property, and royalties.

Some items are considered assets, but the resale value may be well below the price you paid for them: cars, boats, computers, appliances, inexpensive jewelry, and similar items. Try to avoid purchasing these items with borrowed money, not only do those items lose value, but you also waste money paying interest.

What is a liability?

The easiest way to put it is that a financial liability _costs you money_! A liability obligates you to repay borrowed money to another party or costs you money to maintain: if you give someone else money to own an item, it is a liability.

We create financial liabilities and _debt_ when we borrow money to purchase items that we cannot afford. The more money that we owe to others to repay obligations, the less money we have to pay ourselves. Those "must have" items may not be worth the stress that is likely to follow when the bills arrive.

What are expenses?

Expenses, like liabilities, cost you money. Expenses are an outflow of money. Because expenses are normally items or services that we consume, they generally do not have a resale value. Examples of expenses are items such as movie tickets, cable service, furniture, dining out, cell phone bills, etc.

What does appreciate mean?

When an item appreciates, it increases in value.

For example, if you purchase a house for $150,000 and it is later worth $175,000, your house has appreciated or gone up in value.

What does depreciate mean?

Depreciate is the opposite of appreciate. When something depreciates, it <u>decreases in value</u>: it is worth less than you paid. Clothes, furniture, electronics, and toys are examples of items that will lose value by the time you get home. Shopping can be fun, but be careful not to spend money on items that depreciate without paying yourself first.

What is a contract?

A contract is when you enter into <u>a legal agreement that is enforceable by law</u>, either in writing or oral. Keep in mind that it must be a *legal* agreement. You cannot hire someone to steal a television and expect to have the agreement enforced if he fails to deliver.

What is default?

A financial default is when you <u>fail to repay your legally binding contract</u> within a specified time.

What is a repossession?

A repossession is when you *fail* to meet your financial obligation and <u>the lender takes back their property</u>. If you stop making your payments as agreed, you are in default and the lender has the right to seize their property.

What is credit?

What is credit? In reality, credit gives us the ability to buy the things that we really cannot afford. Credit is <u>a loan that creates debt</u>, or the ability to receive goods or services before you pay. A furniture store may allow you to take home merchandise with the agreement that you will pay in the future.

What is a line of credit?

A line of credit is the maximum amount of money that a financial institution is committed to lend to a borrower.

What is consumer credit?

Consumer credit is borrowed money or credit for personal or household use such as major credit cards, bank loans, gas credit cards, store credit cards, auto loans, installment plans, etc.

What is a financial obligation?

A financial obligation is when you have a legal duty to repay a financial debt. If you borrowed money, you are responsible for repaying that money.

What is debt?

Debt is created anytime you borrow money. If you want your money to grow, keeping your debt low is important.

What is consumer debt?

Consumer debt indicates that *you owe money* for items (liabilities) that you purchased with consumer credit. We normally purchase items with this borrowed money that *depreciate in value.*

What is secured debt?

Keep in mind that secured debt means that the creditor (the person or company that lent you money) can take back their property if you default on the loan (fail to repay as promised). The most common secured debts are for homes and cars.

So, if you fail to keep up with your mortgage payments, the lender can foreclose on (take possession of) your home. Or, if you fail to meet your financial obligations, the lender has the right to take back the vehicle.

When you purchase secured items with borrowed money, it does not belong to you until you make the final payment! The lender purchased the item for you, but you must buy it from them!

The joke is on us. The creditor really owns the property, but we get the responsibility of ownership: the upkeep, taxes, providing insurance, and everything else that goes along with true ownership.

What is unsecured debt?

With unsecured debt, the creditor <u>does not have the right to repossess the property</u> if you fail to repay the loan. The creditor *does* have the right, however, to sue and try to get a judgment against you. Merchandise purchased with credit cards falls under the category of unsecured debt.

Taking out a second mortgage, also known as a <u>home equity loan,</u> to pay off credit card debt is common; the thought of people doing this makes me really nervous. You should think long and hard before taking out a home equity loan to pay off unsecured debt such as loans or credit card bills!

Remember that creditors <u>cannot</u> take back items purchased with unsecured debt without a judgment. A creditor can, and probably will, take back property purchased with secured debt if you default or fail to pay as agreed. If a creditor takes possession of the property, they will try to resell it to regain some of their money.

What does bankruptcy mean?

There are many types of bankruptcies. The most common is a Chapter 7, in which the courts declare that you are unable to repay your creditors. The rules for this legal procedure can be very complicated and should be discussed with a professional. Keep in mind that filing for bankruptcy can be harmful to your credit. If possible, it is always best to repay what you owe.

What does principal mean?

When you borrow money or take out a loan, the principal is the initial amount of money that you borrowed, before interest and fees are added.

For example if you borrow $500:

$500 - principal or loan amount

$ 25 - application fee

$ 75 - interest

$600 = Total (random numbers used for representation only)

What is interest?

Interest is the cost of borrowing money or receiving credit. Sometimes when we take out a loan or use a credit card, we forget to factor in the *cost* of borrowing money. I think of finance as a game: the goal of creditors and lenders is to make as much money in *interest* from me as possible. My goal in the game is to run my household efficiently while paying very little interest.

What is simple interest?

Simple interest is the amount of money you pay for your loan. Simple interest is common with auto loans; there is normally no penalty for repaying the loan early.

What is a prepayment penalty?

A prepayment penalty is sometimes charged by the lender or

creditor for paying off your loan before the due date. A prepayment charge defeats the purpose of repaying your account early, which is to save money on interest. Always check to be sure that there is no prepay penalty in your contract.

What is compound interest?

Compound interest means that you <u>earn money on the principal and on the interest</u> that you previously earned.

What is a fixed-rate interest loan?

With a fixed-rate loan, your interest and monthly <u>payments remain the same</u> during the life of the loan. Because your payments stay the same each month, it is easier to create a budget.

What is an adjustable-rate interest loan?

With an adjustable-rate interest loan, your <u>payments will rise or fall</u> depending on the interest rates in the economy. Be careful when considering an adjustable rate loan.

What is a teaser-rate loan?

With a teaser rate, the lender may <u>discount the interest</u> at the beginning of the loan to give you lower payments. Eventually, they will phase out the discount rate and your payments may increase to a rate that you cannot afford.

What is a combination loan?

With a combination loan, you arrange with a lender to take out <u>two separate loans</u>. For example, you may take out a loan for the down payment of a home, normally 20%, to avoid paying private mortgage insurance and a second loan at 80% for the remaining price of the mortgage.

What is a balloon payment?

A balloon payment is a <u>large lump sum that is normally due at the end of the loan</u>. Balloon loans can commonly be found in mortgage loans, so always read the fine print. The balloon payment covers the loan amount that the payments do not cover. Balloon payments are often used to keep monthly payments low.

I had a friend who did not realize that her auto loan included a balloon payment because she did not read the contract. After making payments for four years, she learned that a large payment was due. She could not afford the balloon payment, and the lender repossessed her vehicle. I felt her pain. If I thought my tears would have made a difference, I would have cried with her. It was a painful lesson to learn, but hopefully it taught her a valuable lesson.

What is predatory lending?

Predatory lending is the practice of convincing potential borrowers to take out <u>overpriced, high-interest loans</u>, when they qualify for standard loans. This is a reason that educating yourself is important before you sign any contract. Do not put blind trust in a stranger. Predatory lenders target people with little financial knowledge. Do not be a victim.

In Robert Kiyosaki's book *Rich Dad, Poor Dad*, he writes, "The world is filled with talented poor people. All too often, they're poor or struggle financially or earn less than they are capable of, not because of what they know but because of what they do not know." Take the time to learn. I cannot tell you enough that the use of knowledge is powerful!

Chapter Six

Breaking the Cycle:

<u>Your Kids and Money</u>

"Tell me, and I forget.
Teach me, and I remember.
Involve me, and I learn."

Benjamin Franklin

Breaking the Cycle
"If I Only Knew Then, What I Know Now..."

Consumer spending in America accounts for nearly two-thirds of the nation's consumption, playing a major role in the health of the economy. Our government not only depends on, but also encourages consumer spending on goods and services. I sometimes scratch my head and wonder if that could be a reason for not teaching financial management in schools? Keep us uninformed, keep us spending?

Since the probability of financial literacy being taught in schools is unlikely, as parents we have no choice but to step up and take charge of educating our children. Up to 85% of high school students do not have *basic financial skills*. That is a scary thought when you consider that most of them will be on their own in a few short years. Kids today may have more money to spend than we did at their age, but their ability to manage money is no better. Remembering the financial mistakes that I made at that age is one of those times when I can only imagine the benefits of knowing then what I know now. I shake off those regrets and remember that it goes back to what Maya Angelou said, "When you know better, do better."

We do not have the power to turn back time, or to change the choices that we made in the past. What we do have is the opportunity to make better choices today to improve our financial future. We also have the power to break the cycle when it comes to our children by giving *them* the information that they need to make better choices. If we give them the right tools and direction, our children can learn from our mistakes instead of walking blindly in our footsteps — spending every dollar that they earn, with no concern for the future. We can help our children build a stronger financial foundation.

Unfortunately, our children have no idea of the amount of financial power that passes through their hands every year. They are spending close to $200 billion annually, making them perfect targets for advertisers; they are young, impressionable, and in control of vast amounts of money. Because they are not at the most generous stage of their lives, they are spending most of that money on themselves, buying items that will have little to no benefit to their financial future. What are they buying with all that money? Our kids are spending large sums of money on items that they use for a short period and discard: trendy clothes, electronic gadgets, video games, cell phones, the latest ring tones. They also enjoy eating out, the latest music and movies, purchasing hair and personal products, and other forms of entertainment.

Where Our Children Go, Advertisers Follow
(Billion-Dollar Targets)

One of the biggest threats to the financial stability of our children is marketing companies and advertisers. Depending on their television exposure, our children can expect to watch at least 100 commercials a day, and more than 40,000 a year. Companies are spending about $17 billion a year targeting children between the ages of two and 17; one thirty-second commercial has the power to create brand preference in kids as young as two. No place is off limits when it comes to marketing. They even follow our children to school, enticing them to buy unhealthy snacks and drinks, with no concern for the increase in childhood obesity. Up to 98% of televised ads targeted to children are for foods that are high in fat, sugar, or sodium.

By the time our children learn to stand and take a few steps, they become fair game for advertisers. Before most children start school, advertisers have them convinced that they need a particular brand of sugar-filled cereal to start their day. They beg, plead, and promise to clean their room for a month in exchange for the latest toy advertised during one of their favorite programs. Advertisers are even encouraging our children to do what is known as the "nag factor" or "pester power."

Not only are marketing companies doing research on the spending habits of our children, but they are also doing research on the parents. This is where the *nag factor* and *pester power* come into play. It seems that if our children pester or nag us enough, we will eventually give up and grant the little darlings their request: rewarding them for getting on our nerves! The bad news is that 55% of our kids say that the nag factor and pester power have worked for them. You will be interested to know that it takes an average of nine times of pestering and nagging before we give in to them. Some of them are forced to try us as many as seventeen times before they get the desired results. A few really persistent ones admitted going as high as fifty times before their parents gave in to their begging.

When my daughters were still in elementary school, their best friends lived next door. One day while we were visiting, I noticed that there were seven different boxes of cereal on top of the refrigerator. I asked my neighbor why she had so many different brands of cereal. She informed me, with a sigh, that her son would not leave the grocery store unless she purchased his favorite brands. When it comes to cereal commercials, companies spend about $237 million a year advertising to our kids, typically with lively cartoon characters.

I was surprised that a child could have so much power over the way adults spend their money. When I was growing up, it was uncommon for children to request, let alone demand, certain toys or food items. We ate the food that was prepared for us and played with the toys that were given to us. I met other parents who purchased items at the request/demand of their children. As a recently single mom, I could not afford to have my daughters influenced by advertising to the point that they would begin to make requests for particular toys or food items.

That was when I decided to talk with my daughters about commercials and advertising. I learned that children are very smart; getting them to understand advertising was not difficult. It was close to Christmas, and I explained to them that they would start to notice an increase in toy commercials. They did notice the increase, giving me the perfect opportunity to talk with them about advertising.

We discussed how the job of an advertiser was to convince people to buy things like toys and cereal. After our talk, whenever my kids saw a toy commercial, they would yell, "Mommy, it's another advertisement on the television, trying to get us to buy toys!" Find your own way to introduce the topic of advertising and marketing to your children. Knowledge and parental guidance are powerful tools to use against the people who want to take advantage of them. We also have the power to reduce their exposure to commercials, by simply turning off the television.

Passing Down the Consumerism Mentality

or

Financial Empowerment

Another threat to the financial stability of our children is a lack of involvement by parents. Parents set the standard when it comes to financial decisions and the lifestyle we choose. Children, on the other hand, learn what they live. If they grow up watching us consumed with shopping malls, fashion, and spending money, they will join the masses and become over spenders expecting instant gratification. Consumerism is the preoccupation with the acquisition of goods. The problem is that our children will begin to measure their self-worth by the things that they buy. People sometimes turn to credit cards to purchase items that they cannot afford, creating a false sense of prosperity. Children in elementary school are even feeling the pressure to keep up with friends when it comes to the latest clothes and CDs, already feeling the need to emulate the children of the Joneses.

To achieve the goal of looking prosperous, we have become a society attracted to affordable payments. Brainwashed by sellers to believe that if we can afford the monthly payments, we can have it all: the expensive cars, exotic vacations, and, of course, the granite countertops that we cannot live without.

The consumerism mentality has created massive consumer debt that has exceeded two trillion dollars, with the average American doing their part with 7.6 credit cards. More than 40% of Americans are spending more than they make: spending, on average, $1.22 for every $1.00 that they earn. With that in mind, also consider that personal bankruptcies have doubled in the last ten years, proving that we cannot afford to keep up with the Joneses.

When we allow our money to control us, instead of controlling our money, we dig ourselves deeper and deeper into financial chaos with the stress spilling over and touching every facet of our lives. The divorce rate is up to 50%, and financial distress is named as a major cause of marriages ending. This cannot be the path, or the *American Dream* that you want for your children. I know it is not what I want for mine!

It is never too early or too late to start instilling good financial habits into our children. Figuratively speaking, we may have to drag the older kids kicking and screaming to get them to rethink their spending habits. Living in the richest country in the world has given us a false belief that we can afford anything that we want. If we cannot afford to buy it outright, we can simply take out another loan. Understanding why America has the lowest savings rate in the developed world is easy when you take into account our lifestyle.

As parents we have two choices: empower our children to take charge of their finances or pass down the "buy, buy, buy" mentality. We owe it to our children to teach them the simple rules that will make life easier for them. It is clear that our school system is not set up to teach our children how to handle money: most of us are credit card-carrying proof of that fact.

Because we hate to say no to our children, we have created mini images of ourselves that believe that they are entitled to everything that they want: *and the little bundles of joy want it now*! It is time to introduce our children to reality. We know our children better than anyone, and whether we like it or not, they will eventually be in charge of their own finances. They will be creating debt, buying homes, starting families, and making important financial decisions. The million-dollar question: Have we prepared them to make healthy financial decisions?

Bill Cosby said, "Humans are the only creatures who allow their children to return home." Because of poor financial decisions up to 24% of adult children move back home with parents. I love my daughters tremendously, but I also enjoy the peace and quiet of my home now that they are out of the house. I welcome, and encourage, my children to *visit*. However, I enjoy watching old black-and-white movies and listening to *my* favorite music without someone changing the station. If we teach them to build a strong financial foundation, we will decrease the chances of them returning home, over their heads in debt, with dirty laundry and empty wallets. I remember when I was a little girl the entire Tyler family would visit my grandmother for the holidays. My grandmother would always say with a tired smile as she waved goodbye, "I love to see you come, and I love to see you go."

Bringing Home Baby
(An Expensive Bundle of Joy)

The cost of *raising a baby* gets more expensive every year. According to the United States Department of Agriculture, you can expect to pay from $140,000 to $280,000 by the time your baby reaches the age of 17. This does not include the cost of college or if your child remains in your home after the age of 17. Your family income, marital status, and location will also affect the cost of raising your child.

It is never too early to start saving for your child's future. If I could go back in time and retrieve some of the money that I spent on unnecessary toys and clothes, I would be a happy mom. This is *another* one of those times when I think to myself, "If I only knew then what I know now." I would not have wasted so much money on things that my children did not need and do not remember. Those toys and clothes eventually ended up in secondhand stores or yard sales — it was money wasted!

I know that resisting the latest toys and clothes hanging on the racks are hard for new parents, imagining how adorable your new baby will look in those outfits. I had the same thoughts when my children were babies, thinking only of the moment instead of the future. You must fight the impulse to buy every cute outfit and new toy. Chances are, your baby will outgrow the outfits and grow tired of the toys before you can pay the credit card bill.

I rarely see children wearing the white walking shoes that my children grew up wearing when they were young. My brothers and I also grew up wearing those white walking shoes. When they got scuff marks, you would just wipe them off and pull out the white shoe polish and within minutes they were as good as new. When they outgrew the shoes, you would have them bronzed for the mantle. Most new parents are embarrassed for their tots to be seen wearing those shoes. Instead, parents purchase the latest name-brand footwear to match their kids' outfits, paying up to $100 for a pair of shoes that their toddler may outgrow in a month or two.

Children need security more than they need the latest shoes or outfits. Do yourself and your children a favor and start saving and investing some of that money. If you purchase one less toy or outfit per month, you can buy a savings bond or invest that money for your child's future, giving your baby a financial head start. By the time your child starts kindergarten, he or she can have a nice financial foundation or a closet full of old clothes and broken toys.

College and Credit Cards
(Setting Our Children Up to Fail)

For most of our children, going away to college is their first experience with independence. With the anticipation of college life ahead of them, and the hopes and dreams of their families on their shoulders, they are off to begin a new life. Parents across the country are taking their children to schools to experience that life and to become educated adults. Some colleges lacking scruples allow credit card issuers to target our children, encouraging them to sign up for credit cards.

Before we can even drive off campus, vendors begin hounding our children with offers to apply for credit cards. Some schools permit credit card vendors to line the halls with tables covered with t-shirts, pens, and cups. Companies often use cheap gifts to entice college students to apply for credit cards. Those so-called gifts could eventually cost our children thousands of dollars and damaged credit.

Companies are using every trick in the book to persuade our children to become hooked on credit cards as soon as legally possible. Why are our jobless, or at least financially challenged, children targeted for credit cards? The goal is to tap into their future earning potential and to create card loyalty: they want our children accumulating debt for life with their company.

Because it is the first experience with credit for many of them, they may not pay attention to the terms associated with the card: making them more likely to incur late fees, pay high interest rates, and only pay the minimum amount due on the card. More importantly, they may not realize that the financial decisions that they are making can affect their future. A negative credit score can affect everything they are working so hard for, such as buying insurance, purchasing a vehicle, employment opportunities, or renting or buying their first home. Seventy-six (76) percent of our college kids say that they wished we had prepared them to handle their financial future.

Eighty-five (85) percent of college seniors have at least one credit card; the average student has four cards and more than $4,000 in credit card debt. Our children, like most of us, assume we need credit cards for emergencies. Some students do use their credit cards to help with tuition and books. The problem is that only a small percentage of purchases by college students are used for emergencies. Instead they are using the cards like cash to purchase items such as:

- fast food
- bottled drinks
- coffee
- junk food
- clothing
- electronic gadgets
- smoking habit
- personal care items
- CDs/DVDs
- entertainment/trips
- cell-phone use
- living expenses
- partying with friends.

These are not emergencies, and they are not worth creating debt to buy. Our children do not need to spend years paying for burgers and fries!

My Own Little
<u>Credit Card Junkie</u>

Long before my youngest daughter went off to college, we warned her about the dangers of credit cards and creating debt. During her junior year at college, however, she applied for and received her first credit card. I found out about her "dirty little secret" by chance when the card issuer called my home to inform my daughter that her payment was past due. Instead of getting my child, they got mama bear. I quickly confiscated her credit card just $20 shy of her $1,000 limit, and only weeks before they raised her limit by another $500. I have to admit that she gave the card up without protest. When I searched her spending history (with her permission), it turned out that most of the charges were at fast-food restaurants and local convenience stores: most of those purchases were for soft drinks and other miscellaneous items.

My daughter was a full-time student and worked less than ten hours a week at the college bookstore. The credit card issuer gave her a $1,000 limit when she had a difficult time paying her monthly cell-phone bill. Making only the minimum monthly payment and often paying late, they increased her balance to $1,500. She was a credit card issuer's dream customer, paying high interest, late fees, and over the limit charges. My first thought was to pay the balance off for her, because I hated the thought of her paying interest and fees. I decided she should learn the hard way about the pitfalls of credit card debt (she is still making the minimum payment on that card).

It is not only our responsibility, but also our duty as parents to arm our children with as much financial knowledge and training as possible. It is up to us to encourage them to seek information. There is no shame in ignorance. The shame is in remaining ignorant when information surrounds us.

Tina's
Credit Card Statement

Example of my daughter's statement with "no new purchases or cash advances."

Account limit at the time was $1,000

Account Summary:	January
Previous balance	980.65
Payment (minimum)	-30.00
New purchase	.00
Cash advance	.00
Protection fee	+ 7.98
Finance charges	+ 14.50
New Balance	= **973.13**

(7.52 went toward her balance)

Account Summary:	February
New balance	973.13
Payment	- 30.00
New purchases	30.00
	(late payment fee)
Cash advances	.00
Protection fee	+ 7.98
Finance charge	+ 14.50
New Balance	= **995.61**

(7.52 out of 30.00 went toward balance)

Account Summary:	March
New balance	995.61
Payment	-30.00
New purchases	+ 60.00
	($30 late fee/$30 over the limit fee)
Cash advances	.00
Protection fee	+ 7.98
Finance charge	+ 14.50
New Balance	= **1,048.09**

A Different Path for Our Children
(A Path Less Traveled)

Like most adults who grew up without financial training, I learned the hard way about money management and consumer debt through trial and error. As you know by now, I knew absolutely nothing about credit scores, credit cards, or interest rates. I applied for credit cards because the salesperson offered me a gift, or because I was with a friend who was applying for a card. By the time I realized the harm that I was doing to my finances, I already had the typical 7.6 credit cards, an auto loan, and two furniture store accounts. I was paying 14% interest on the auto loan and more than 24% on each credit card.

When it comes to our financial decisions, I think more than a few financial advisors would agree that most of us have been traveling through life without a plan. If you drive across the country without a map, you are destined to get lost along the way; the same can be said for financial planning. After years of traveling without a plan and creating more debt than I could manage, I finally learned that having a plan and setting goals makes life easier. Once we realize what it takes to bring financial stability to our lives, we may be reluctant to give up our reckless spending habits. We may be forced to admit that we enjoy the lifestyle that credit affords us: the big house, fancy cars, trips, flat-screen televisions, and other toys. Giving up the good life can be difficult, even if that life is borrowed.

As parents, we play a major role in the financial behavior of our children. According to Randy Russac, a specialist in child psychology at the University of North Florida, children take on parents' attitudes before the age of six. Teaching children at a young age to develop healthy financial habits is crucial in helping them avoid the financial problems that plague many adults. Our children come into the world debt free, and parents can lead them in their rise or fall. If your little one is old enough to understand that money has the power to purchase toys and candy, then they are old enough to start developing good money habits. If your child is old enough to ask for money, they are old enough to start learning about borrowing money. Most banks and credit unions offer accounts designed for kids, sometimes even offering prizes as incentives to save.

Children can and should be taught to be just as comfortable in a bank both saving and investing, as they are in stores spending money. Children love to learn; they love games and challenges. If we can combine their love of learning with fun and good financial habits, we can create financially responsible adults. The Internet has websites devoted to teaching kids of all ages about money, using interactive games and worksheets. It is also full of information for parents on how to raise money-smart children.

By raising children who are financially literate and responsible with their money, we can give them the freedom to reach for the stars. If they are not spending half their lives dealing with consumer debt and financial stress, they will be free to use the creative side of their brain to flourish. Instead of focusing on their next paycheck, we can give them the power to soar. Give your children the freedom to enjoy life without the stress of how they are going to pay for that life.

The stress of debt can easily lock away your dreams and talents. By eliminating my debt, I eliminated my stress, and that gave me the freedom to reach for a dream that I never knew I had! Give your children the financial freedom to unlock and achieve their dreams.

<u>The Power of Choice</u>

I would like to thank you for joining me on the first steps of my journey. What my travels have taught me and I hope that I have passed along is that life is all about the power of our choices. Living with debt is a choice and not our destiny. Spending beyond our means is not the American way — it is a choice. To think beyond today and plan for tomorrow is a choice. In life we will continue to find ourselves at crossroads. It will be the choices that we make at each intersection that will determine our future.